THE TOUR

Christopher Keane

STEIN AND DAY/*Publishers*/New York

First published in 1974
Copyright © 1974 by Christopher Keane
Library of Congress Catalog Card No. 73-90708
Designed by Jeannette Jacobs
Printed in the United States of America
Stein and Day/*Publishers*/Scarborough House, Briarcliff Manor, New York 10510
ISBN 0-8128-1667-6

for Barbara Grace

Acknowledgments

My gratitude and thanks to all the players and officials on the pro tour whose advice and guidance made this book possible; Gary Cosay, friend and agent, who every writer should have as a friend and agent; my parents, Jack and C.C., for a million great things; and the Wilson Sporting Goods Company who made my first set of clubs.

Contents

1
How It Begins

Of all the major sports, golf is the quintessentially private experience. At six in the morning, scruffing through dew and grass, a single figure can be seen, bag slung over his shoulder, hat pulled down over his eyes. Suddenly, from out of the rough, another figure emerges, scraping dirt off his three iron as he makes his way toward the green. Then another, a chubby kid with freckles, walks up from behind the green toward the round white object a few feet from the pin.

The first two men are older, in their fifties; the freckle-faced kid is fourteen, and he's beating hell out of the ancient guys. It's the fifth hole and he's been in match play with them, low ball wins the hole. The difference is that he's playing against both of them, one ball against two, and he's three up.

It's been like this for three years—the kid has taken his father and his father's friend for a ride ever since he turned eleven.

His name—Roger Bradey. Schoolboy champ of Ohio at thirteen and Florida High School medalist at sixteen, seventeen, and eighteen. He drove the ball on the average of 280 yards, had a scratch handicap and was the hope and dream, the golden boy, of Fort Lauderdale Country Club and most of the eighteen others in the area. Roger had it all going for him: sponsors willing to put up the $400 a week it takes to survive on the tour; the most promising career in all of Florida; and an uncanny short game that matched the strength of his long game. But he was never even close.

The closest he came was assistant pro to Arnold Palmer when Arnie was at the Country Club of Miami. Last I heard he was a club pro in some obscure town in California, married, with one kid, a new Chevy every year, and a fading dream. The pro tour eluded him, just as it had each year since he graduated from high school. Like the popular cheerleaders and all-conference halfbacks, who shone in their senior-high heydays, Roger was at his own zenith, and then fell away.

I remember his calling me at five in the morning, just after we'd delivered the Sunday *News.*

"Let's go," he'd say. I grabbed my sticks and met him at Fort Lauderdale Country Club's first tee. The North Course. We had to tee the ball up high to avoid hitting the soggy grass. We still lost twenty to thirty yards on the drive because the air was so heavy that time of the morning. But it was the best time to play—we had to press to get the distance. Then, after playing that early in the morning for nearly three months, we learned not to press so hard, but to concentrate on accuracy. As a result, we became what the country club mint-julep crowd called "excellent young golfers."

In the summer of 1962 we sent out letters to every club of any significance in the state, challenging amateurs and pros alike to come to Sunrise Country Club in Fort Lauderdale to play. They could name the stakes. In June we started on the light side. Hundred-dollar Nassaus—hundred on the front side, hundred on the back, and a hundred for the match. With automatic presses at another hundred a shot. By the end of July we were in the thousand-dollar bracket.

To this day, I have always said that if we had not played gin rummy in the afternoons after the morning matches, we would have been very rich. As it turned out, when the final tally was in, we had $5000 between us. Not bad for a couple of kids from Stranahan High, the state champs every five years out of eight. But not so good for a couple of seventeen-year-old hustlers who stood to win close to $30,000 if they'd stayed the hell away from the gin table.

Roger and I used to talk about how some day we'd both be on the pro tour, probably banging two irons into the final hole at Augusta, tied for the Masters on the last day. Thousands would be standing around eighteen, waiting, applauding as the two of us, buddies to the end, marched the last hundred yards, heads down, pushing along a few feet ahead of our caddies. Then after we'd talk about it we'd walk out to the course and see that gallery in our imaginations and play some of the best golf of our careers. It was not long before we got a taste of the real thing.

Sam Snead, when he was head pro at the Boca Raton Club in southern Florida, was asked to play a charity match for a heart-disease foundation. The chairman of the event, who was also the chairman of the Plantation Golf and Country Club, suggested that two of his young players meet with Snead and a partner of his choice. He chose Cary Middlecoff. The match was set, and Roger and I spent sunrise to sundown lugging our cheap canvas bags down the fairways. A couple of crewcut teenagers gonna take on the pros. We spent a full week, at least thirty-six holes a day, checking out every inch of the layout.

The course was a few miles from home, so we drove one day in Roger's beat-up '54 Ford pickup and the next day in my '49 Chrysler convertible, the "Bluebird," with cement blocks in the trunk to make it look racy.

We tore the course up. On the first day, before we developed any real strategy, Roger came in with a 67 and I was right behind with a 70, two under par. We had it made; that is if we didn't freeze up against Snead and Middlecoff, the Slammer and the Dentist.

I borrowed my father's Buick on the morning of the match, picked up Roger, whose blond, muscular body sat fidgeting on his front porch, and took off for Plantation. The crowd was already large when we pulled up.

"Weird, isn't it?" Roger said as he sat low in the seat next to me, picking the dirt out of his driver with a tee.

"Are you nervous as I am?" I asked.

"Oh no," he lied.

Snead and Middlecoff were on the first tee talking with some officials. We walked down the long asphalt path toward them, confident, spikes clicking along under us. We were not that confident. Petrified was more like it. We stared straight ahead, nodding occasionally when someone said hello. How the hell was I going to hold the driver when my hand was shaking so much? Roger walked beside me in his usual slump-jog, shoulders bent, stomach thrust forward, his light blue Penguin shirt and Arnold Palmer slacks tight around his body. He looked like a pro. I was in black and white, a la Gary Player, and my white, tassled Foot-Joys, just three weeks old, looked good as I watched them moving out in front of me, one after the other. Our golf gloves hung from our right rear pockets. There we were, the Cream Team, out to take these big-time boomers for a ride.

Roger was the main attraction; he'd won pro-ams and the state title twice. He knew there were sponsors in the crowd looking him over, waiting to get their cash into his future. I kept saying over and over in my head: We're seventeen! Seventeen!

On the first hole, a three-hundred-seventy-yard dogleg right, Snead blasted his drive over the right bunker and left himself fifty yards from the hole. Middlecoff was thirty yards behind him. It was my turn. I had my driver out and stepped up to the tee. The only sound came from Roger, standing ten feet away, whispering, "C'mon, Chris."

I overlapped my hands around the pro grip, bent my knees, put my weight on the balls of me feet—all the stuff you learn when you begin playing, but which I thought about very carefully at that moment. I addressed the ball and, bringing my club straight back, I put everything I had into the swing, sending the Titleist in a high arch toward the trap. It started to draw a little, curving over to the left, dropped in the center of the fairway, about two hundred and sixty yards out. Applause. Whew! If every shot's got this kind of pressure, I thought, I won't make it to the second tee.

Roger got up and bombed his over the trap, ending up just a few yards behind Snead. There was a solidity in Roger, a confidence, that convinced everyone of his ability. He approached a shot like a hunter would his prey, systematic, trained, absolutely confident. There was no doubt, as he stepped up to the ball, that the shot would be there in the fairway. This assurance, however, was also his nemesis. When he blew a shot, he went berserk, as if his mechanism short-circuited. Clubs went flying into the air, profanity spewed from his mouth. And it usually took him three or four more shots to get back on the track. That wasn't the case with that first drive, though; it was a beauty.

Snead talked a lot, about everything, to anyone who would listen. And most of them did. He especially talked to Roger, who talked not at all. Once he hit the course, dirty words under his breath and a lot of "way to go's" were about it. While Middlecoff and I marched toward our balls—with him laughing and gabbing and me scraping and bowing—Snead was on Roger, asking questions, giving advice.

It took me three holes to realize two very important things. The match was only superficially the two of us against the two of them; it was really Middlecoff against me and Snead versus Roger. The short hitters against the long ones. As soon as we stepped to the first tee, our opponents knew that Roger was the one to get to, and Snead was doing his damnedest. After a while Roger began avoiding him by rushing ahead or falling behind, by standing off to the side of the tee, or going to the water fountains for drinks.

Their plan was to get Roger irritated, and it was working.

The second realization, which followed close on the heels of the first, was that this match pulled us out of the small-time amateur tourneys and jammed us right into the big time. Snead and Middlecoff actually made their livings from golf and, like all successful businessmen, they knew all the angles. It's not just hitting a ball that makes golf pros, it's the time in between the shots, the extra edge, that finally brings in the bacon. That particular round was going to make or break the magic for Roger and me.

Our game plan was similar to theirs—Roger would go long and for the birdie; I'd play safe and for the par. It had worked well in the practice rounds. Neither one of us had been over par during our last fifteen rounds.

By the fifth hole, a dogleg left with a huge trap in front of the green, the match was even. But something was wrong. It was match play, low ball wins the hole; I was two under, while Snead and Middlecoff were one under each. Roger was two over par and very gloomy. Somehow he had to let out the pressure.

He usually slammed a four iron against a tree or screamed "Fuck!" twenty times, but not on that day, not with two thousand gallery members crowding around. And especially not at a Heart Fund Benefit. No way. I certainly couldn't carry it myself. I knew that. And not having major support from Roger, I was convinced that my two under par would not last forever.

On number six, Snead flew a two wood eight feet from the pin. He lay two on a par five. Middlecoff and I were down the middle. Roger had shanked his second shot into the rough. Snead sank his putt for the eagle and they went one up.

We had to do something drastic, so I started talking to Roger about Doris Engels, affectionately known as the "Town Pump," who at sixteen had lost count of the number of guys she'd "banged." Doris was special; she'd only sleep with boys on minor sports teams—golf, tennis, and swimming. No response. Then I tried cars, and then Bimini, where we were going the following week because we sold the most newspaper subscriptions. Silence.

As we walked down the eighth hole, Roger turned to me and said, "What if we concede the match?"

"What!" I shouted, and looked around to see if anyone had heard his ridiculous statement.

"No, I mean it."

"You piss me off," I said, and walked on ahead.

It wasn't that bad of an idea, since after the front nine we were three down with as much chance of winning the match as Snead and Middlecoff had of losing it. The two upstart high-school kids didn't have a prayer. A few dozen gallery members left the ninth green and decided to spend the duration getting loaded in the clubhouse.

At number ten I took Roger aside and told him something I'd been saving for just that kind of situation. I let him know that I'd bet my last $100 on the match, the money I'd broken my back for on the paper route. He was furious.

"Whaddya crazy?" he screamed at me.

"I guess so," I mumbled, and sulked off toward the tee.

Roger was up third and drilled his drive three hundred yards over the right trap and down the tree line. A good back nine start. I pulled out my own driver, a Freddie Haas signature club I had made by Irving King of Shreveport, with the biggest head in the game. It was so enormous it looked more like a trudgeon than a golf stick. I faded it around the corner, two hundred and fifty yards out. Roger won the hole with a bird. Suspecting that something had happened to make Roger go through a major transformation, Snead ambled over and began nibbling at his ear again. This time Roger talked back, laughing about this and that and chewing the fat with the West Virginian.

It was not until many months later when it hit me: Snead was not rattling Roger to win the match. Instead, he was putting him through a kind of basic training, prepping him for the pro tour, getting his head into the right space. Snead, and everyone else who had seen Roger play, knew he was prime material—he had strength, finesse around the greens, a good-but-growing-better short game. What he needed were nerves, and control of them. That's what Snead was after: to give him a taste of the high pressure and an ability to handle the down times. In short, not to give up when his game was off. And more importantly, not to let guys like Snead, the fast-talking, down-home needlers, break his concentration. Because that's what he'd get on the tour, from the moment he set foot in the clubhouse to the last hole on the final day. Snead was teaching Roger one thing—how to cope.

On the fourteenth, a very short but mean par three with woods in the back and a lake down front, the tide shifted. When Roger dropped his shot into the water, I didn't want to watch. After a moment I felt a hand on my shoulder. It was Roger, and he was smiling, his red, sunburned face and short blond hair a few inches from my nose. "That's the last bad shot," he said, and leaned even closer. "We're gonna win this thing." We made a deal. If I'd win one of the five remaining holes, he'd take three. I said sure, why not? We halved the fourteenth. The pressure was on.

Snead and Middlecoff were cool as ever as we approached the tee. They gabbed to the spectators and joked together, as if they had the match aced. That irritated me, and I told Roger.

"We're gonna make 'em sweat, Chris," he told me. "Just watch."

He stepped to the tee and drilled one about three hundred down the right side. As he picked up his tee he lifted his head and winked at me. All right, dammit, here we go. I also belted one, my best drive of the day. Suddenly there was electricity in the air—the gallery caught it, Snead and Middlecoff did too. We were on our way. We'd win the match. There was no longer any doubt. What's three down with four to go? Chickenshit. The time was now.

Roger sank a thirty-footer for a bird and the gallery went wild. Even though I was calm on the outside, my internal system went bananas, as if Roger and I had hooked into the magic. Finally. We were golden.

The pros who make it on the tour—and not just *to* it—are the ones who, like a backstretch horse, close fast. Palmer did it in his heyday: "Eight strokes back at fourteen, Palmer wins by two" the news headlines read, or "Nicklaus wins sudden death." It's the come-from-behind action that separates the pro from the al-most-pros, when the pressure is so great that it shifts him into high gear. Explosive, relentless, he chases the pack, passing them one by one, until he clears the line and picks up the big money.

And then there's the timing. It's almost as if there's a small gearbox in the pro golfer's brain that clicks on when the time is right, when he's got to make his move. Sometimes it's circum-stance—three down with four to go, as we were—while at other moments the magic does it. Something mysterious like a small voice tucked back in the brain that says, "Now," or something ob-vious like a beautiful woman in the gallery for whom, in a split second, you decide to win.

For Roger, as he told me later in his prophetic voice, "It was fate."

When Roger blasted his tee shot around the corner on seven-teen, I could tell by his demeanor that he loved the whole thing. He was on the tour at that moment, and he had just proved it. I could see him, just as he could see himself, in Los Angeles for the L.A. Open, the first stop in January on the tour. And then the Masters, the Open—all of them. It wasn't that he was cocky; instead it looked as if he knew he belonged in the big league, right along with Snead and Middlecoff, who by the seventeenth he was beating on strokes.

His mood shifted only slightly when Snead rolled in a thir-ty-footer for a par. We were two down with two to go.

I had promised Roger a win on one of the last four holes. It had to be seventeen, a short par three, because eighteen was always my nemesis. Roger, on the green about twenty-five feet away, was closest of the foursome. I was off in the weeds to the right.

We walked together toward my ball. "Just get close enough so I can go for the bird," he told me. It was all very familiar, the two of us strolling to our tee shots. Shades of the Great Summer Hustle of the previous year when we'd map out the shots days in advance. Not that they'd turn out that way, but at least we had something to base our game on.

It's do or die on this one, I said to myself as I pulled the wedge out of my bag. Snead was in my line and marked his ball. The gallery was still. Roger squatted down on the apron, looking as if he were in prayer.

I came under the ball cleanly and it swept out of the tall grass on its way toward the pin. It hit ten to twelve feet in front of the pin and bounced, bounced and rolled in! My wedge was already in the air when it dropped. Roger was running across the green toward me with his arms open.

"Great fucking shot," he said. "We'll *both* be on the tour this time next year." I believed him. It was a great shot, my greatest yet, I thought. The best ones are never made on lazy Saturday afternoons when four guys bat the ball around for kicks and a few bucks. They're made in situations like that, when the tension's up, when everything's on the line. That's when everything comes together. I promised Roger a hole and he got it.

The word had gotten back to the clubhouse that we'd made a comeback, and the green was already surrounded when we hit the eighteenth tee. It's the kind of hole you hate to meet on a hot, scorching day. Long, flat, and uphill, it looks more like a runway at Salt Lake Flats. I was down the middle, Roger belted his about two seventy, and Snead and Middlecoff were in good position.

Snead pulled out a four and put the ball thirty feet to the left of the pin. Middlecoff was by this time sweating profusely—but probably not about the match. It was hot as hell. He pushed his three iron a little too much and ended up off the green, forty yards to the right. I punched a three on the apron, and Roger, with a six, lofted his shot on a dead line toward the pin. It hit eight to ten feet behind, the hole, grabbed the turf and, with some good English rolled back toward the pin. It stopped a foot and a half away and the crowd went crazy.

It was going into sudden death, unless by some miracle either Snead or Middlecoff holed out. Not much chance of that. Snead had an almost impossible putt and his partner was too far off the green, on the side of a small hill.

Middlecoff, looking as if he wanted to end the match in a hurry, walked up to his ball and, with a wedge, dropped it on the green. The ball hit something—a divot—and started off course, on the high side of the pin. It kept rolling, but then curved back down. It was still ten feet from the pin and moving when I knew we had lost the match. The ball curved down, down and in.

The congratulations were not enough, nothing was. Roger and I were superdepressed. Our worlds had collapsed. We were heading for Edge City. Chicken Little was right. The worst part was that we had to wait around for the awards ceremony.

All the time we sat in the clubhouse listening to the speakers expound on heart disease and the wonderful golf match we two fine, young players had given the big, tough pros, all I wanted was to hop in the car and take off for the beach with Sally, who loved me so much she'd sometimes carry my golf bag for thirty-six holes at a clip.

It was that day—that defeat—that took Roger out of the running for the pro tour. The "pressure was too much," he told me. I said it was just a freak thing, that we'd lost to two of the top pros in the world by one stroke, and that we still had a few years training till we hit the big time. I told him also that I'd lied about the $100. I didn't bet it; all I wanted was for him to get moving. "Didn't you have any confidence in us?" he scolded me.

He disappeared before the ceremony was over and was in deep depression for weeks afterwards. During the time following the match he lost his first and only high-school tourney.

It was a long time before he broke out of it, and it took eighteen holes with the pros to put him in it. I sometimes wonder how he's doing out there in California, what he feels when one of the big tournaments, like Pebble Beach or the L.A. Open, comes to town.

But this is not Roger's story; it's about the winners, the ones who made it, the stars. Yet there are hundreds of thousands of freckle-faced kids who can beat their fathers all day long and dream about all the U.S. Opens in the world. Some of them break through the fantasy to enter the ups and downs, the big money, and the flash of the world's greatest traveling sports circus, otherwise known as . . . The Tour.

2
A Round . . . and a Round: Behind the TV Scenes

The television camera mounted high on its platform behind the eighteenth green zoomed down the fairway and picked up the lumbering figure of Jack Nicklaus marching towards his drive.

Chris Schenkel, in his mellow, fireside chatty voice, no longer tried to make the tournament a head-to-head battle. It would have made no sense; Nicklaus had already clinched it.

The other ABC commentators—Jim McKay, Bill Flemming, Frank Gifford, Keith Jackson, Byron Nelson, and Dave Marr—had focused on the Golden Bear since he first came into sight back on thirteen. Schenkel was in awe of the hero of golfdom, just as the 20,000 gallery members and half a million TV viewers were.

This was the last of the Big Four tournaments. The Masters had been played months before; the U.S. and British Opens were memories. And so, it seemed, was this, the 1973 PGA Championship at Cleveland's Canterbury Country Club.

One by one the challengers—Bruce Crampton, Mason Rudolph, and Don Iverson—had fallen back as Nicklaus charged through their ranks, exploding their dreams of taking first and making them concentrate on grabbing the runner-up spot.

The PGA had become a battle for number two.

Throughout the two-day, five-hour television coverage, the viewers were treated to a short history of the PGA Tournament, biographical sketches of the top players, tight camera shots on their faces wrought with emotion, long shots down the emerald green fairways, and Byron Nelson's words of wisdom on the game of golf and the men who played it.

Television gave us all this: the emotion, the insight, combat on the playing field, a piece of the iceberg above the waterline.

What the television audience never sees and is seldom made aware of is the substance behind the scenes. What we see on television and read in the newspapers and magazines are only small islands in the world of professional golf.

One of the first major tournaments I covered was the 1973 PGA at Canterbury. For many reasons. Not the least of which was the preparation that goes into a tournament of that dimension. Much of the nose-to-the-grindstone work happens weeks—even months—before the camera equipment is rolled onto the course; some of the work is still going on while the cameras are rolling; and some even happens after the TV people pack up and go home.

The television viewer seldom, if ever, sees this, and often is not aware that any of it is taking place.

What follows is a sort of potpourri of certain elements organic to the tournament itself, elements without which the TV audience would never hear the announcer's voice or watch the action on the course.

The PGA, the Vols
and a Bitch or Three

To put together a tournament like the PGA takes thousands of people and hundreds of thousands of dollars.

Dozens of committees have been set up the year before, manned either by club members or volunteers.

The PGA is one of those tournaments, like the U.S. Open, that is played on a different site every year. Consequently, the preparations are enormous in comparison with permanent-site tournaments, where technical jobs like laying cable and setting up a communications network have been taken care of years before.

For most Canterbury CC members the honor of having been chosen to host the PGA overcame any inconveniences they might have had to put up with. For others, however, it was a real pain.

Smack in the middle of summer, in early August when most people have extra time to play golf, no golf could be played. The course was closed for more than two weeks, and the members had to go elsewhere to whack the ball around.

Another burr in their behinds was the fact that when they did go to the club it was filled with construction men, advance publicity writers, television vans, and a hundred other things one doesn't like to find on his home course.

"I am rather unhappy about the whole thing," said one member. "Not only do we have National Golf Day, which takes up the course, but now this. I realize that much of what National Golf Day makes goes to charity, but the PGA proceeds go right into the PGA kitty.

"I cannot say that I'm not proud of what's been done. The publicity for the course is all well and good, but when it interferes with my playing time, I don't like it. How would you like it if all of a sudden a movie company came into your home and used it for two weeks of shooting? You wouldn't. I wouldn't. I don't like it at all."

Another member who was for the idea explained it this way: "There are so few courses in this country chosen for a national championship with the importance of the PGA. We are not forbidden entrance to the course; we do the same things here we've always done. Except play on the course. The Shaker Heights Club has been nice enough to allow us to play there during the tournament. I feel little or no inconvenience. Compared to what Canterbury gets out of having the PGA, the small sacrifice is well worth it."

Worth it? It had better be, for the PGA, which organizes the tournament, the Canterbury chiefs of staff, like course superintendant Bill Burdick and host pro Duff Lawrence who take care of the logistics, for the writers who combine tradition with up-to-the-minute coverage, and for the pros themselves.

Then there are the men and women of the Professional Golfers Association who originated the tournament and run it from the executive level.

Being PGA secretary was not enough for Henry Poe; he was named chairman for the fifty-fifth PGA National Championship. Poe's primary duties at Canterbury were to see that the 700-plus volunteers at the club and the neighboring courses meshed their activities with more than one hundred members of the PGA of America serving as observers, rules committee, registration workers, and a dozen other groups.

Poe sits at the apex of the organizational staff and runs the tournament with all the precision and planning of a Harold Geneen greasing up his own machine over at IT&T. "Our operation," said Poe, "should operate on the same solid business principles as any major industrial corporation. We must be certain that today's problems do not become tomorrow's impossibilities."

There are four routes a pro golfer can take when decision time comes around: he can bust his hump, get his head and game together and, like a Nicklaus or Palmer, go for the big money; he can come to the realization that he can't hack it on the tour and if there's an offer, he becomes a club pro and teacher, retiring in later years into St. Petersburg obscurity; he can quit altogether and teach phys ed in high school; or he can climb through the ranks from labor into management. Henry Poe traded in his Foot Joys for Bostonian leather, a pro shop for an executive suite.

His father ran the Hillandale Golf Course in Durham, N.C., with Henry as his assistant. From there it was only a matter of time before he served under Craig Wood at Winged Foot in Mamaroneck, N.Y., a class course and major credit. The next year, 1940, he took over from Byron Nelson as head pro at the Reading CC in Pennsylvania.

From 1957 through 1959 he was the national PGA vice president and two years ago was elected—on the first ballot, no less—to take over as secretary.

"Bill Clarke may be the PGA president, but Henry really runs the show," a PGA official told me. "While many men in that capacity would settle for being the power behind the throne, Henry won't. He's everywhere, and from what I hear Bill Clarke is getting edgy."

In a tournament like the PGA, with its grandeur and national prominence, the problems are enormous. A major one has to do with volume. Specifically, the 700 volunteers who are there to cater to the needs of just about everyone.

The Vols, in their light blue and yellow costumes, drive cars—hauling the pros, PGA members, press, and anyone else who looks remotely important to and from the motels, airports, hot-dog stands and booze parlors. They work for free, sometimes fifteen hours a day, and hardly ever bitch about it, except to one another.

"I just don't know who's who anymore," one of them said as she hauled Ray Floyd, Ed Sneed, and me back to the motel. "They tell me where to go, and I do. I don't know who's getting into the car. For all I know they could throw me out and drive it to Chicago."

"Have any trouble?"

"Not me, but some of the young girls have been approached."

"Accosted?"

"What?"

"Accosted. You know, jumped."

"Oh, there's been talk. I've overheard things from some."

"Like what, for instance?"

"They told me not to say anything."

"Who told you?"

The smile was still on her face, but her eyes told me she didn't like my third degree. End of conversation.

The next morning I caught a ride to the course with one of the "young girls."

"I heard you girls have been approached by some of your riders. Did you expect that sort of thing?"

"Sure."

"How come?"

"They said it might happen. I kinda like it. I mean, it's flattering."

"Have you gone out with any of the golfers?"

"Last night."

"Terrific, who with?"

"Well, here we are," she said with a smile.

"Right. Thanks a lot."

The Cops

The security force, not only protects the pros, the gallery, and the course, but also maintains the integrity and well-being of Canterbury and all that it represents.

Charm rides high on the Canterbury links. Skidmore, Gilligan, Walter Kelly (Shaker Heights mayor) are names that dot the social register, and they all belong to this ritzy, middle-American-chic club.

Everyone wears white shoes out there, not because Nicklaus and Player and company brought their flashy off-white shoes into the game years before, but rather because white dominates. It's elegant against the pastels of their slacks, shirts and skirts.

The folks there speak with perfect inflection. The rumor about broadcasters getting their crisp, authoritative voices from the Midwest is true.

Canterbury. Very English. Old school. Airy, pleasant, civilized. They smile and say, like the Californians, "Have a nice day"—but they mean it. They treat life the way they do their children. Conventional and cheery.

Standing outside the press tent were two women, Burns Detective agency guards, who were there to check badges. The security force at the PGA, unlike the one the week before at the Westchester Classic, blended with the environment.

The contrast between New York and Ohio was obvious by the way the guards looked. At Westchester they were policemen from the county sheriff's office. They wore guns strapped to their belts, night sticks hung by their legs, and a row of bullets wrapped around their waists. As if someone were going to walk off with the tenth tee. At Canterbury, in keeping with the charm and elegance, there were no arms, no sticks, no threats of impending disaster. And a quarter of the force were women.

The security guards' main duty is letting into the grounds those who belong and keeping out those who don't. They are also responsible for checking the grounds at night for prowlers who might hate golf enough to dig up some greens, which has happened quite a bit around the country. Most people write off green-choppers as pranksters, kids who have nothing better to do. Others don't see it that way.

Bill Talbot, a Kansas pro up for the PGA who as a kid did his share of ruining greens, saw all kinds. "I was a hell raiser when I was young. My parents had a house on the course, so a couple of friends and I used to take rakes and dig up the tees and greens. It was something to do, and we got up early the next day and watched the first foursome come up. Just to see their expressions when they saw the condition of the greens.

"But I'll tell you, some nights we saw old guys out there doing the same thing. They looked crazy. Most of them had clubs, irons, and they whacked away till half the green was dirt. Never seen anything like it.

"I figured maybe they had a bad round or took an eight on a par three for money, something like that. It's all psychological. Maybe they couldn't afford to play."

The security people are there to protect against that, though most of their worries have to do with stray gallery members wandering into a restricted area or getting into a fight. The reason for so much security is the TV equipment, hundreds of thousands of dollars worth of cable, cameras, and electronic gear that a team of high-class burglars might walk off with.

The Diggers

Most of that equipment is aboveground, in the ABC vans and the dozen or so trailers surrounding them near the eighteenth tee. What allows all of it to operate is below the surface, known only to a group of specialists who spent months laying it. Four and a half miles of cable still weaves its way throughout the course.

The cable, developed by Bell Labs and Western Electric, contains a gelatinous substance that hardens immediately upon exposure to air. One Ohio Bell official explained it this way: "If there's a little cut in the cable—for instance, like what a muskrat did on the seventeenth fairway a few days ago when he bit his teeth into it—the material oozed out of this cable; and it immediately hardened, thus keeping water out and preventing all sorts of other problems."

It was the first time the cable was ever used and it will remain a permanent fixture on the course. "The only thing we're concerned with," the official went on, "is the weather. If it rains, we could be in some trouble. A bad storm, a lightning storm, something like what happened at Oakmont at the U.S. Open when lightning hit that TV tower and knocked out a hundred-seventy-five pairs of wires; if that happens, we'll spend twenty-four hours fixing it up."

This cable business is no ordinary thing. The system is equipped to carry 900 simultaneous conversations. On the opening day of the tournament no less than 3000 calls came in or went out of the club. On the third day it was over 5000, not including the lines from the press tent, which on a heavy day means another thousand or so.

"The real problem," says the official, "is in the golf tournament itself. It's spread all over the place, on many different acres. You never know what's going on from one place to another. You suddenly get a young kid coming out of the clouds as the leader and everybody in his home town is calling wanting to know how Johnny is doing."

"What are you prepared for?"

"The worst. We're putting in probably anywhere from fourteen or eighteen hours a day out here. I've got a foreman and four men on the main crew that's doing all the installation work. I've got a special service crew that's doing the special-service circuits, the special ABC circuits. And I've got another crew doing the regular TV circuits work, the microwave, and the balancing of all these circuits through micros."

"In other words, you're handling—"

"Everything."

The big plus about leaving the cable in is, of course, not having to take it out. In addition, "Let's say we've got maybe 170 members out here and they suddenly decide wouldn't it be fun if we had a big score board to show who's doing what. Simple, we could put in a scoring line and record scores for all the holes. The people back in the clubhouse would know where they stand at every minute. It wouldn't cost very much to hook it up and think of the great time everyone would have!"

There's nothing like having your own leader board to spice up the club championship.

The man who takes care of the course from an office deep in the clubhouse is a thirty-two-year-old baby-faced guy who looks more like a decathelon star than what he is—the golf-course superintendant. Bill Burdick made three trips to Oakland Hills, where the 1972 PGA was held, to check out the operation. He wanted everything to be perfect for his own at Canterbury.

Gone are the days of the scruffy old groundskeeper who learned his trade by hanging around courses all his life. Burdick and his twenty-five men, like Don Shula with his offensive and defensive units, work on the platoon system. Burdick himself went to Penn State to study things like plant pathology, entomology, agronomy—subjects that old greenskeepers never heard of, much less practiced. At the University of Massachusetts and Kent State, Burdick studied landscape architecture, horticulture, agricultural engineering, nursery operation, accounting, public relations, marketing.

What was once his primary job—maintaining the playing condition of the course—is now only one of his responsibilities.

"As for knowing about accounting procedures," he said, "it should be remembered that we are handling a great deal of money. We also are operating on a budget, so it is important that we know about purchasing. For example, the seed market fluctuates drastically. Knowing when to buy can save a great deal of money, and what you can save on seed makes money available in the budget to spend on other things."

Other things—meaning the holes themselves. In 1973 the average cost per hole reached $6,554, $305 more than in in 1972. Like the rest of the game, maintenance costs have risen 73% over the last ten years.

Whatever happened to old Pop Walker who used to hike out to the greens every morning to set the pins and chew the fat with his assistant—if he had one? Burdick estimates that 75% of the country's course superintendents are between twenty-five and thirty-five and have similar educational backgrounds to his own. "Up until ten years ago," he said, "golf-course superintendent was a job that paid very poorly. I don't know how they lived on what they made. But since then the pay had multiplied three times. It has become quite a field.

"While twenty-five years ago only one college offered a course in turf-grass management, now it is being offered in colleges throughout the country. The University of Massachusetts had eighty applicants for only forty-five openings in its last course. There now is a fear that so many are coming into the field that the job market might be flooded."

Another person the TV audience will not see on the telecast but who figures significantly into the operation of the tournament is the host golf pro.

In 1968 a Canterbury CC committee was in the process of filtering through 100 applications for the job, only the fifth in the club's history. One of the recommendations read, "He is one of the finest young teaching pros in the country." It was signed Jack Nicklaus.

"He" was a thirty-one-year-old, ex-All-Army-Team member from Iowa who chose the host pro route over tour play because he hated to travel. Duff Lawrence came to Canterbury after spending two years as head pro at the New Orleans CC.

Lawrence was instrumental in getting the PGA to Canterbury. Along with general tournament chairman Bob Watts, he went to PGA officials and talked them into bringing the tournament in.

That Lawrence is a top teaching pro is only part of the reason he was brought to Canterbury. He picked up a lot of that Southern charm and savoir faire down in New Orleans, and it was this charm and his ability to endear himself to those who counted in the golf world that clinched the job.

Some host pros are loners; others have no tact when the going gets rough. Lawrence is always cool and congenial. Bob Watts mentioned two of Lawrence's qualities and qualifications, both of which made a lot of difference when his name came up: "He is a gentleman and a Christian."

Which does not mean that non-Christians weren't considered for the job. None applied. The same thing goes for membership at Canterbury. Of the ten members asked if any non-Christians were part of the club membership, none could think of any. "But we don't discriminate."

Have any, say, Jews, applied for membership? I asked them.

"Not that I recall."

The same policy applies here as it did in a small southern Pennsylvania town I once visited. I noticed there were no blacks in town and wondered why. "Well," said a shopkeeper, "we ain't prejudiced about Negroes up here."

"That's good."

"Know why?"

I didn't.

"There ain't none."

Duff Lawrence bounced around the grounds during the tournament, bumping into old friends and making new ones. One thing Lawrence wants more than keeping the members happy during the tournament, or placating the PGA, or selling equipment in the pro shop is good press.

Golf writers no longer demand to be treated well, they expect it. Lawrence knew that and was right in there pitching and wooing. The best place for that kind of thing was the press tent.

If anyone has kept the game of golf alive, more than the players and the PGA and the manufacturers and the TV, it has been the scribes. In the giant circus tent near the course entrance, writers like Lincoln Werden of the *New York Times,* Dana Mosely of the New York *News,* the wire-service people and the newspaper-syndicate boys bang on their portable typewriters and send the play-by-play over the wires to their newsrooms. Some writers actually spend more time on the tour than the pros, who take a break every once in a while. Someone once said that every day is a vacation for the golf writer—if you call living out of a suitcase year after year a vacation.

In a tournament like the PGA, tradition plays a major role. Whether it's the equipment manufacturers in their brightly colored sports coats, the classic Scottish architecture of the course, anecdotes from the past, or a stretch drive by one of today's heroes, it's all written down. Television will show you the great shot, but it's soon forgotten in the midst of other great ones. In newspaper morgues lie the accounts of all the great shots. You only have to ask for them.

The tradition of Canterbury, as told by writers, goes back to 1922, when the course first opened for play. That date began a history filled with some of the most interesting stories to come out of golfdom.

One of the "Canterbury Tales" found Walter Hagen winning his first major tournament at the 1932 Western Open. Hagen is also the only man to have won five PGA championships. Jack Clowser, a Cleveland sportswriter for forty-three years, tells how Hagen, three shots behind Olin Dutra with four holes to go, put his game into high gear:

"The final round was played with a near gale sweeping off Lake Erie and lashing the high ground at Canterbury. . . . At the fifteenth hole (sixty-ninth of the tournament), both were on the green in two. Hagen was about twenty-eight feet away. Dutra was inside, about twenty-four feet. Just then a cowbird flitted across the green. Walter grinned. 'I could use a birdie now, couldn't I?' he asked the gallery.

"Hagen rolled in his birdie three amid wild applause. Dutra, shaken, not only missed his own try for a birdie, but also muffed a three-footer, carding a bogey five. His lead was cut down to a single stroke.

"On the enormously long seventieth, which was then at six hundred fifteen yards, Dutra half-topped his second and took a bogey to Hagen's five.

"Then came Hagen's coup de grace. The seventy-first hole was being played with the markers at the extreme rear, two hundred twenty-five yards. Hagen selected a one iron and hit a screamer that covered the flag all the way, stopping six feet short. He hit his birdie putt into the center of the cup and nailed a one-stroke lead which held up through the final hole."

At the 1929 U.S. Amateur at Pebble Beach an Englishman, Finley S. Douglas, then president of the United States Golf Association, made waves with this comment: "The press is becoming too large. The only persons who should be coming here are the wire service reporters."

Writers made such a stink about this statement that their readers played hell trying to find out who was winning the tournament.

A few years later, at the 1936 U.S. Open at Baltusrol (Springfield, N.J.), the press accommodations were miserable. It was not difficult to figure out why the room they were given was dirty, airless, and poorly lighted. It was in the basement under the clubhouse. The writers, probably believing that they deserved no better, waited ten years to get out of the cellar.

It took a glass-enclosed dome overlooking the eighteenth at the 1946 PGA in Portland to make them realize what a shaft they'd been getting all those years. Fred Corcoran, PGA tournament director at the time, announced to the press one night that they should continue getting what they deserved and form the Golf Writers Association of America.

Corcoran recalled that when he stood up for the announcement, the writers, who were supplied with enormous quantities of booze, didn't much like the idea. Two of them, the secretary and the president, would have to do a lot of extra work, too much, they felt, for any rewards they might get.

Russ Newland of Associated Press had to go to the bathroom, and was elected president *in absentia*. When he came back from the john the news hit him and he promptly appointed Charles Bartlett of the Chicago *Tribune* as secretary, a job Bartlett carried to his grave.

Then there was the time, at the 1967 Masters, when the press was barred from the locker room. The story goes that Ben Hogan had objected to a picture of him in the Augusta paper. The picture itself was fine; what Hogan didn't like was the bottle of Scotch sitting on his locker for all the world to see. Just before press headquarters exploded, Ben rushed over there and explained that all he did was casually mention it to a couple of friends. The ban was immediately lifted.

At the 1970 U.S. Open at Hazeltine, Minnesota, a tray of cold cuts had been placed in the locker room with a sign: FOR PLAYERS ONLY. When Will Grimsley of the AP got there to interview a player, the tray had already been ravished down to a couple of pickle slices. At one point, when Grimsley reached down and snatched up one of them, he was confronted by an irate member who told him to unhand the pickle and get out.

A high-level conference took place, out of which New York *Post* writer Gene Roswell came up with a plan. He bought a plate of salami and hauled it over to the locker room where he began eating it in front of the member who had screamed at Grimsley.

What Roswell didn't know was the matter had already been taken care of. His fellow reporters, some pros, and members watched with fascination as he ate the entire greasy mess. The member he was out to get stood there mute.

At the 1973 PGA, one of the most exciting events was captured by a Cleveland *Plain Dealer* writer who wrote that another writer from the Newark *Star Ledger*, when asked what he wanted most to do at the tournament, answered, "Find some girls." Not only was the *Star Ledger* writer misquoted, he also didn't find any.

The press tent is a mixture of all the elements in golf, the brain of the tournament, where information from every faction and from all parts of the club finally ends up and is filtered out to the public. At one end are wooden tables with typewriters, information supplements, and old news releases hanging out of trash baskets. Against the wall is the leader board, where three or four scorers chalk in the most recent tallies. At the other end of the tent is the interview room. The leaders are brought to a table elevated five feet above the floor to answer questions put to them by the journalists.

The interview room is where the golfers' personalities come

alive. When Johnny Miller told the twenty writers that the PGA "tricked up the greens," it was news. Hot stuff. There was a real story.

The writers scrambled from their chairs back to the other room and banged out the piece. The story in this case was fast, on-the-spot coverage, front-page stuff, recording a piece of history. Of course there was a deadline, the pacemaker of wordplay. There was a certain nervousness when the clock read ten minutes to go.

Sportswriters are the real mailmen of journalism, for nothing short of sudden death or a major holocaust will prevent the news from leaving the writer's head for his public.

80,000 Strong

While the journalists slammed out their copy in the tent, out on the course, lining the fairways and surrounding the greens, was a sea of bodies that added spark to the tournaments. Without the gallery, which the camera picks up but treats as what the networks call local color, the game itself would lose a lot of momentum.

Golf is the only major sport which has its fans traveling right along with the players, joking and talking with them, watching them close up. Add to that the fact that in golf there is no standard uniform—except for the glove and shoes—it means the gallery wears what the golfers do. Mingling is the name of the game.

The week before the PGA, at Westchester, I stood by the caddie yard watching a man dressed in a sky-blue hat and yellow shirt, standing in the midst of the gallery by the tenth hole like a cop directing traffic.

I watched him for a good five minutes, during which time at least fifty people walked up and asked him something. With each person the man thought for a minute, looked at a piece of paper he carried in his pocket, and then pointed in one direction or another.

His name was Bob Allen and his specialty was galleries. He'd seen them all, at most of the tournaments on the East Coast. There he was again at the PGA.

"Well, I'll tell yuh," he said, after I dragged him out of the way, "I know what people need at a tournament. Directions. Nobody knows what the hell's going on. They don't know who's who most of the time, what the scores are, who'll be where at what time. I know."

"How?"

"The sheet," he said, pulling from that rear pocket a list of the day's pairings and tee times. "I check the place out beforehand and stand around a conspicuous area. Most of these jokers couldn't care less who's winning. They want to rub elbows with the favorites. And when they see a great shot, terrific, but they'd rather see the reaction of the guy hitting the ball. That's what the gallery looks for when they come out for the live coverage."

Allen said he's been doing it for years. "What exactly have you been doing for years?" "I love golf, and I want to make sure everybody's got a fair shake at what's happening."

He doesn't walk around with the golfers because his arthritis acts up after two holes. "I bought one of those things couple years ago"—he pointed to a cardboard periscope vendors sell to the gallery members who stand in the back. "It's good for short guys, you know."

"Like yourself," I offered.

"Right." He didn't like my firm grasp of the obvious. "What they don't understand, the short people, that is, is they can sneak through and get a front-row seat. Those periscopes are dumb. You might as well watch at home. Short people, by the way, are usually the first ones on the course when it opens to the public. Look around early tomorrow and you'll see the average-height person is about five three. They're the ones on the apron first. They sit there all day. They bring their wives and kids and a picnic lunch and camp out. It's like going to the beach for them. They love it. Short people think a lot more than tall ones cause the tall ones are always in their way, so they gotta figure out a way to kill the problem."

One thing odd about Mr. Allen was that whatever question I asked, he didn't need it. He had an answer ready before I said the first word. Whether the answer had anything to do with my question made absolutely no difference. When I asked him about the gallery members who run across the fairways when a player's hitting, I got this:

"You know why most people are out here? Broads. They don't come to watch the game. Look at that one." He aimed his finger at a young blonde in a halter. "Great! She's fantastic. Why not spend a few bucks to watch that? Who knows, you might get lucky. The broads are here for the same thing."

Mr. Allen (which he wanted to be called) has no neck, a double chin that runs from his jaw to his chest, two constantly moving, chubby arms, a bowling-pin body, and a hole in the side of his mouth from smoking too many cigars.

Despite his rapid-fire mouth, he is a loner. He knows few people since he spends most of his time fishing. Now that he's retired. He'd already been to nine tournaments during the year, and plans on going to half a dozen more.

"Don't believe everything you hear about the pros not liking galleries."

"I haven't heard that much."

"You will. Like the time the kid fell out of the tree here in Cleveland. They loved it. 'Course they also worried about him. Some of the people are nasty, but there's one thing you always gotta remember. The gallery never roots against a player. You ever hear booing on a course? Never happens. When a good shot goes up they're all for it.

"They love the game more than the players winning or losing. Golf's the best sport for the sport itself. Sure, you want to see your boy come in first, but if somebody beats him out, so? It was a good match. Golf is too easygoing to get hyped up on one pro. How many people you seen working up a sweat over a pro? I'm not talking about his family, just the average guy."

Mr. Allen had finished talking. He shoved the sheet back in his pocket, tipped his cap, and walked off toward the first tee.

While most gallery members are orderly, some are not. The biggest problem for the pros through the years has been cameras clicking in the middle of their shots. At Westchester the week before Tom Weiskopf ran into a 35mm Nikkon.

He'd come in with a 69 on the third day, taking a bogey six on the eighteenth. He later told the press that "The cameramen were not responsible for my bogey on the last hole." When he was first asked about the incident, which had obviously upset him, he replied, "No comment."

But he added, "I have a recommendation. It is well known that there are signs on the course and at the clubhouse reading 'NO CAMERAS.' People with cameras should be put off the course. It's frustrating. They try your patience. When a marshal asks them to stop they take pictures anyway."

Weiskopf told the press it wasn't their fault, but as one official who was there said, "Tom was forced to back away from his tee shot on eighteen when a camera went off. His second shot went into the rough behind a tree, and when the cameraman began taking his picture Weiskopf called the marshal over. 'He's bugging me,' he told him. The marshal chased the cameraman and his friend off. They escaped by disappearing into the gallery.

The credentials of a *Newsday* photographer were later lifted.

Weiskopf didn't win the tournament, even with his last-day charge after the quadruple bogey. It didn't throw him off that much. At the PGA he came in with a 283, good for $7,312. Not bad for a week's work.

Behind the scenes in golf, the management running the show, the course personnel taking care of the logistics, security people, technicians, writers, and the hundreds of others who contribute their time and effort, are what the tech crews are to the Broadway stage. They make it possible for the stars to do their thing in front of an audience.

Call them unsung heroes, say they never get their due, make a case for their obscurity. Everyone knows that without them there would be no show, no prizes, no TV. No big-time golf.

3
The Gold Screen,
or Stroking
for Dollars

It wasn't so long ago that Alan Shepard hit a six iron on the surface of the moon, thus making golf the one and only cosmic sport. The event was witnessed by a record crowd, thanks to the supreme recorder of news throughout the universe—television.

Once upon a time, golf used to be a quiet, unobtrusive sport, sheltered from the public by large iron gates and spiffy white fences undulating around two thousand acres of plush green. Only those who could afford the equipment and fees played this weird game whose objective, it seemed, was chasing a little white ball for ten miles.

It used to be when golf was covered by the press, when it was covered at all, we could spot a single column five pages back in the sports section, with no byline, but with (AP) or (UPI) nudged in against the dateline.

Most readers passed over it; some read it with the same

interest they'd give the obituaries; the buffs hung on to every word. That was two decades ago. Things have changed.

Enter the tube.

Television viewers were treated to their first golf event, George S. May's Tam O'Shanter World Championship, in 1953. The finish couldn't have been better.

Chandler Harper had a virtual clinch on the $25,000 first prize as he stood off the eighteenth green with a 279 tally. The only guy with a chance to catch him was Lew Worsham. His chance was a slim one.

The final hole was a long par four. Worsham's drive left him one hundred yards from the pin, and he needed to get down in two to salvage a tie. He lifted a wedge high in the air, drawing it slightly from right to left.

A huge gallery stood around the green, while millions more were glued to their black-and-white, slightly fuzzy TV sets, hoping for but not really expecting a miracle. They got it.

The ball skipped into the hole while Chandler Harper's heart skipped a beat. If television golf was going to make a splash in the video world, it couldn't have made a better dive.

The following year, George May hiked the purse up to $100,000, half going to the winner. It was ironic that Bob Toski took it all that year, for it was television that helped push the prize money to $50,000, and it's still the tube from which Toski makes a living as the "expert" commentator on Hughes Sport Network, which televises more than a dozen tournaments each year.

It took a major oil company (Shell), seven years later in 1961, to break down the fences even more and rush in the truckloads of TV equipment. Shell's Wonderful World of Golf crept into weekend time slots with the first golf series. At Wentworth in London, Dai Rees nipped Jerry Barber 74-75 to collect $7,000 first money. Total prize money for the nine years the show was on the air was close to $1,000,000. Shell pulled out in 1970, due mostly to mounting competition from the regular tour, and the series died.

Shell's contribution to the game—the ninety-two films were

watched by at least 15,000,000 people—was the single most powerful shot in the arm for the sport. The series not only encouraged the average duffer to play more and the novice to pick up his first club, it also made it clear to the PGA and tour-sponsoring groups that a helluva lot more prize money had better be offered if they expected the country's top professionals to play on the circuit.

Shell's reasons for getting into the marketplace initially sounded like a corporate computor readout, but the message has prevailed: "The program was designed to create a favorable image of Shell by describing significant contributions made by the company to the cultural, social, and economic life of the countries in which the matches were filmed. The objective of the commercial messages was to portray Shell as part of a worldwide organization with a concern for progress and human welfare . . . and to leave the impression of the benefits which the company brings to consumers in the United States as a result of its international association. Golf was chosen as the theme because the sport was growing rapidly, with millions participating, and tens of thousands of new players joining the ranks every year, thus creating a growing audience. Golfers as a group are above average in income and influence, and include influential individuals who not only consume petroleum products themselves but influence their companies' purchases in these products."

Other sponsors clamored for time on the tour, willing, as they always are, to pick up on a good thing.

The sponsors know that golf is not as popular as football or basketball, but is still a major market for their products. Their target is the upper-income viewer, the guy who would buy a Cadillac instead of a Ford, who'd fly across the country rather than drive, who'd drink a Michelob over a Pabst.

Playing off the idea that golf is a money sport, that country club members are generally high on the executive level, and that everyone else who watches would love to be there, banks and insurance companies dump millions into golf telecasts, along with high-power conglomerates like IBM and AT&T.

Irv Brodsky, press representative for ABC Sports, mentioned advertisers in a particular product category who want to be solely identified with a series of golf tournaments or with a specific event.

"Mutual of New York has identified itself very closely with the Tournament of Champions, to a point where we acted as intermediary. They first were interested in television sponsorship. They then became so interested in the tournament that they're now underwriters, or co-underwriters, and put up the prize money. They simply buy up the heaviest piece of advertising weight in that tournament.

"ABC runs the Tournament of Champions an hour on Saturday and an hour and a half on Sunday. In a co-sponsorship, Mutual might have three or four commercials running on Saturday, and of the twelve running on Sunday, they might have five or six."

Another big advertiser in golf events is Chevrolet, who wants to be identified with golf, period. Chevrolet buys into all ABC tournaments. And they buy at a level which allows them to have what the network calls exclusivity.

"Which means," says Brodsky, "we will agree when the deal is made that if they continue at that level, we will preclude other automobile manufacturers from buying into the tournament."

Of course, a lot depends on what tournament he's talking about. The U.S. Open always has a higher rating than, say, the Byron Nelson Classic or the Colonial or the American Classic.

Since golf is, event by event, the most expensive of all sports to produce—equipment, rights, etc., often send the cost over $500,000 per tournament—the average charge to the sponsor is $40,000 a minute. Not a very attractive figure, considering the number of viewers watching, but one of the things golf has going for it is the demographics, the fact that those viewers who do watch are particularly desirable: 90% male, unusual in television viewing except in sporting events, and they tend to upscale in terms of education and buying power.

"Golf also lends itself extremely well to a kind of selling we do," Brodsky added, "and that's what we call total-marketing selling. Instead of having an advertiser buy a unit of time, make a commercial, and shove it in the middle of some show, he links his product to the show itself."

In 1973 ABC had no trouble getting sponsors; the sponsors came to the network. In the mid-sixties though, when advertisers weren't beating down the door, president and executive producer of ABC Sports, Roone Arledge, had to rely on special tactics to get them in. One of the best, still revered as one of the ultimates in the selling game, was conjured up by Arledge and put to the sponsors.

"Would you be willing to pay $20,000 for one minute of the PGA?"

"You've gotta be kidding." The stakes weren't so high then.

"I didn't tell you for a minute of what."

"Don't bother. That's ridiculous."

"All right, then. Forget it. I'll try somebody else."

It didn't cost anything to listen, so the advertiser paused to let this crazy man go on.

"Twenty thousand for one minute . . . a one-minute talk with the President of the United States."

"What!"

"You heard me. On the air. Congratulating the winner, following a spot for your product."

The setup was this. The winner walks off the eighteenth green, the announcer has a short talk with him and then tells the viewers that, after a message, the President himself will be on the line. What advertiser in his right mind would say no, and for a measly twenty grand?

The relationship between the networks and the advertisers does not end with the commercial. The same outfit that buys a minute during the U.S. Open might also, with a little encouragement, buy a minute during prime time. On "Marcus Welby," for instance.

On Monday, August 13, the day after the 1973 PGA at Canterbury in Shaker Heights, the course was empty. But not for long.

ABC invited the advertisers who had bought air time to play on the championship links under the same conditions the pros played during the tournament.

The advertisers were told to bring their major accounts for a one-day tournament, a feed, a few laughs, and some deals if they cared to. The result: everyone would benefit. The network wooed the sponsors, the sponsors wooed their clients.

The network not only gave them a tournament, it provided transportation, a golf clinic, and a chance to play with Byron Nelson and Dave Marr.

The old cliché about the biggest deals being made on the golf course is neither old nor a chiché.

Jack Nicklaus used to take twenty minutes to make a shot, which irritated the hell out of his fellow golfers, the gallery, the TV audience, and the networks.

"And now, Nicklaus will hit his shot to the fifteenth green," said the announcer.

Ten minutes later.

"And *now*, Nicklaus will hit his shot to the fifteenth green," said the announcer.

Eight minutes later.

"And now, Nicklaus will hit his shot to the fifteenth green," said the announcer.

Golf has been accused of being slow.

The players themselves have been accused of being poker-faced, emotionless bores, which makes it difficult for the commentator to announce that so-and-so, at the eighteenth hole, is wracked with emotion. The pro's only wrinkles, it sometimes seems, are on the inside.

Though the networks insist that the man takes precedent over the event, they've gone a long way to lush up his surroundings and make the tournaments look as if they're going a mile a minute.

Pre-tournament publicity is much easier to pull off than trying to make exciting what the viewer might see as tedious.

As far as the golfers themselves were concerned, you could

almost feel the commentators' sigh of relief when Tommy Bolt hit a bad shot. He might explode any moment, just what was needed to get things going. Or when Gary Player, in his black-and-white outfit, bounded up the fairway. Network chiefs offered up prayers the night before tournaments, hoping for leaders with some flash. Few of them were answered.

What to do?

First, the networks started bidding for the winter tournaments. They were naturals for pulling in the most viewers. Harry Jones from Stony Brook, New York, finished shoveling snow at four o'clock Saturday afternoons and shuffled into the living room. He turned the knob to Channel 7 and before him appeared Hawaii. Hula dancers wearing two small pieces of cloth around their bodies, waves tumbling in from far out at sea, seventy-eight-degree temperatures, next best to being there in person. So what if Harry didn't know golf, he had palm trees.

The Neilsens on winter golf tournaments beat the rest of the year by a long shot. We wonder how the golfers can concentrate on their games with so much beauty and action going on.

The networks must be doing something right, or maybe golf itself is doing it. On the following page are the top ten tournaments in 1973 live golf telecasts: The Nielsen data was supplied by NBC and Hughes Sports Network.

As the first ingredient in the plan to capture the TV audience, course location made use of nature in its most attractive stance.

The second ingredient was the golfer himself. How, wondered the networks, could the pro appear more competitive, more rugged—more interesting?

Man against nature came up as a major theme in the late sixties as commentators pointed to hazards the pro could confront: out-of-bounds, bunkers two hundred fifty yards out in the middle of the fairway, rough so deep it looked like a jungle.

Terry Jastrow, a producer with ABC, explained the human-drama angle. "We want to show very clearly what it's like with a guy's expression on his face, either determination before he

Rank	Event (telecast dates)	Network	Homes Reached *
1	Bing Crosby (Jan. 27–28)	ABC	8,420,000
2	Bob Hope (Feb. 10–11)	NBC	7,650,000
3	Williams San Diego (Feb. 17–18)	ABC	6,760,000
4	Hawaiian (Feb. 3–4)	ABC	6,060,000
5	U.S. Open (June 15–16–17)	ABC	5,810,000
6	Masters (Apr. 7–8–9)	CBS	5,420,000
7	Campbell L.A. (Jan. 6–7)	CBS	5,330,000
8	Gleason Inverrary (Feb. 24–25)	CBS	5,120,000
9	Colgate-Shore (Apr. 14–15)	ABC	4,810,000
10	Martin Tuscon (Jan. 20–21)	NBC	4,540,000

* If two rounds telecast, average is listed. The all-time record audience was 9,680,000 homes for 1971 Crosby.

makes a shot or elation or sadness after he's played the shot. I mean, these guys are not just people with fourteen clubs who hit good shots. They're motivated by the same things you and I are, and have problems and hang-ups and day-by-day human problems. That's what we try to point out, because it makes them more readily identifiable to our audience."

In addition to the natural beauty and man's struggle against it, the networks, in their quest for continuity, place heavy emphasis on the story line. "To keep the relative nature of the story as it develops is extremely important," according to Jastrow. "For instance, we try to tell the worth of each shot as it relates to the overall development of the tournament."

Building interest is what sportscasting is all about. To isolate one shot from another only creates confusion, or worse, disinterest in the mind of the viewer.

So Arnold Palmer hits a two iron into the fifteenth green, so what? That the shot is within four feet of the pin, and to sink it means he goes into a tie for first with Nicklaus on sixteen *is* important.

It's the old woulda-shoulda-coulda aspect of the game that matters. *If* Palmer sinks, *then* he goes into a tie. The power of suggestion, the idea that anything might happen at any time right up to the last second, makes golf one of the most volatile of the major sports.

Golf also has some built-in advantages that makes it easier for the commentators to deliver their spiel without losing the audience right away. A great many viewers are golfers themselves, so when Tom Weiskopf took a quadruple bogey eight at the Westchester Classic in 1973, the viewers shook their heads with an "I know how it feels, I've been there myself, Tom." And in the same tournament when Tom staged a comeback, rallying to within a shot of the lead, the audience again felt the emotion of one who had also been in a similar situation.

Another built-in plus the networks have to work with is the sudden emergence of an unknown into the lead. There have been a number of rookies who've forged into the lead after the first round of a tournament, only to falter later on. Forrest Fezler did it a couple of times on the '73 tour. At the 1974 Crosby at Pebble Beach, Gary McCord, who had won more than $80,000 on the mini-tour, grabbed a two-stroke lead on the opening day.

Suddenly, the announcers had a new face to talk about: young upstart taking the bacon away from the big boys. Furthermore, they could talk about the mini-tour, where McCord had done well, and a number of other things which only the rookie has to go through.

NBC's Jay Randolph, who covered the Crosby and Hope tournaments, feels his own interest grows when a young pro makes a splash. "There's more tension in the air, more excitement. The possibility of a young pro taking it all makes announcing a lot more interesting." When McCord blew to an 80 on the third day, the flash was gone. He fell victim to something most rookies experience after their initial round. The little-known pros are usually paired with each other the opening day. If they find themselves within the top five or ten on the second day, they're given a better starting time, which the stars are alloted as a matter of course. Playing with a Nicklaus or Trevino is hard on them. They are thrust into the national spotlight, they feel the camera eye on them, they know the announcers are talking about them. And most intimidating of all, they are playing alongside men whose faces are constantly exposed to the public and whose names are household words. The pressure is too much.

The dilemma of a Gary McCord is hot news, and the networks make the most of it. His first round 65 was good theater, and in the interest of sound broadcast journalism, so was his 80. The fallen hero and all that.

What we see and hear on television is called external promotion or live coverage. What goes into a tournament before air time, and what we don't see during the telecast, has to do with logistics.

Because of the nature of the sports, golf and auto racing are the most difficult of all to broadcast. "It's like televising five or six football games all at once," says Irv Brodski. "Or like the Olympics, where a dozen events are taking place at the same time. But golf is even tougher than the Olympics. First, it's all live coverage, with none of the going back to pick up a pole vaulter or a hundred-yard dash that happened ten minutes before. In golf, you've gotta be on the ball all the time."

Before the actual operation goes into high gear, the networks have to negotiate with the PGA and, sometimes, the USGA. The basic cost of a tournament runs from between $150,000 and $500,000, not including rights, the $100,000 to $150,000 the network has to pay the PGA and USGA. The "rights" mean that the network can broadcast both domestically and in foreign countries. When ABC bought the PGA Championship, it also had to do extras like producing the U.S. Women's Open and U.S.

Men's Amateur, and one USGA event such as the Walker Cup. The network also has an out, since the rights mean that ABC has the first right of refusal.

After those negotiations were completed, ABC started planning for the '73 PGA.

The equipment alone—$3,500,000 per event—makes golf the costliest of all sports events to cover. Compare the PGA with a world-championship boxing match: 100 men and 23 cameras against 5 cameras and 15 men in the boxing arena. In addition, ABC, the PGA and Canterbury CC laid out $500,000 for the four-and-a-half-mile-long cable and communications systems alone.

Two weeks before the tournament began, the equipment was moved in by way of vans, located in a cluster behind the eighteenth green.

One of the most important aspects of the coverage is camera placement. On the par four holes, for instance, there are always two cameras behind each green. What we see on television is something like a funnel approach to sports coverage. On the earlier holes the angles are long, and wide, but as the leaders approach eighteen, the shots get tighter focusing on the players' emotions, their hand movements, their actions and reactions. It's like that opening shot in *Lawrence of Arabia* in which we see a speck in the distance moving toward the camera. As the speck becomes larger we see that it's a man on a horse. Finally, when the horseman gets right up to our noses, we see Omar Shariff in all his splendor.

One thing the networks insist upon is a good finish. If they can't have it score-wise, or with a late charge by one or two golfers, they at least want it to look good hole-wise.

Though most tour courses have terrific closing holes, some do not. In those cases when mediocrity prevails, the networks have a meeting with the PGA. The subject: change the course.

At the Westchester Classic the final holes were rather boring, so the Hughes Sports Network did a little dance and came up with a new arrangement. Critics of this practice base their arguments on the idea that if the natural layout is not good enough, don't hold the tournament on that course. The networks counter by pointing to their need for exciting finishes. Who wants a blasé par four when you can have a fascinating par five? The networks win. After all, they pick up the tabs.

Another bitch heard from viewers and writers is much closer to the nature of the game itself. Frank Boggs of the Oklahoma City *Times* took time out one weekend to watch the U.S. Open and came up with some interesting statistics.

Golf on television, said Boggs, is a game for putters and little else. "Throughout the telecasts viewers were able to witness 244 putts and 158 other-type shots. And, of those 244 putts, 67 were tap-ins . . . Arnold Palmer was televised on 78 shots in all, 45 of them putts. . . . John Schlee was on camera for 46 shots, 31 of them putts." And so on.

Boggs' gripe is a valid one. Why are there so many cameras on the tees and greens, and not on the fairways, where the players have their most difficult shots?

Television doesn't seem to be aware that golf telecasts are both entertaining *and* instructive. It's great to hear Byron Nelson analyzing Gary Player's swing, but what about the time in that same tournament when Player blasted out of a trap, caught the lip, and found himself farther from the hole than he started out? No camera was around to pick it up.

No one is particularly interested in seeing fifty shanks and duck hooks every round, though they're there, nor are we wild about watching Weiskopf dribble the ball twenty yards out of the rough and then slice it into a concession stand on his next shot. Not all the time, anyway.

But if the networks are so interested in capturing the human element, why not do it? The viewers can learn from the pros—what to do and what not to do. Commentators seem almost embarrassed when the camera has picked up a player making a bad shot, and they quickly cut away to another hole.

The fault lies in the network staff who see golf, and other

sports as well, as games played by professionals, people who by virtue of their positions do not make mistakes. If the player is not a hero on that day, the networks would rather not have much to do with him.

The man behind this, the one in the control booth running the show, is the producer. He makes the final decisions, calls all the shots.

Sports coverage is unlike any other form of entertainment in that the producer rather than the director actually runs the show.

Chuck Howard, vice president in charge of program production for ABC, sits behind a bank of monitors, receiving information from his staff and the dozens of spotters out on the course. Once he makes a decision as to where the next shot will be, he simultaneously tells the director and announcers what's on the agenda.

The producer's mind is like a computer; the information is fed to him at such a rapid rate that I wondered how the hell he could keep everything straight.

"Long years of practice," he said.

"But don't you get tired of it?"

"Not really, because there's something new each time. If I were counting pencils, well . . . . But here nothing's ever the same. It's a challenge, really, to keep the show together."

"What about predicting outcomes? More than anybody, you're the guy who knows what's going on out there."

"The mystery. For that very reason—that I can see so much—I have to juggle things in my mind. Where to go on the next shot, and the shot after that. I could make predictions. Who'd listen? My guess is as good as the next guy's."

Terry Jastrow, who also lives in the truck while the tournament's on, feels strongly about changing one aspect of the broadcast—announcers throwing the ball to other announcers.

"I don't think you and I care if Jim McKay throws it to Frank Gifford or if Bill Flemming throws it to Chris Schenkel. We want to know that we're going to the thirteenth fairway and Jack Nicklaus, and then back the the fifteenth and Tommy Weiskopf.

"The producer should say, instead, 'Okay, there's action on fourteenth, the leader's second shot,' Then it can go to Bill Flemming.

"If I were listening on television, I'd much rather hear about the player than the announcer. More interest is created; maybe there's something exciting on fourteen we should know about."

Actual excitement is created in four ways for the viewer: what the audience itself wants to see, what it anticipates; what is happening on the course; and what enthusiasm and knowledge the commentators themselves can bring to the broadcast.

Each network wants to project a certain image to its public; the announcers, more than any other source, reflect it.

CBS, conservative, competent, gives an impression of solidity, a no-fooling kind of reporting that soothes the audience. When Ray Scott, who also does the Hughes Network coverage, Ken Venturi, the expert, and Jack Whitaker, the voice of the CBS Classic, speak into the microphones they're subdued, as if they're part of the gallery who happened to find themselves in the booth announcing. The sport itself, for CBS, holds major focus. The announcers' personalities, though not inhibitive, are for the most part unexciting. The drone of the monotone. When I watch a sports event on that network I usually turn the sound off and put a record on the turntable.

CBS has been fortunate though, especially in golf. Ten years ago it staged a major event in the CBS Golf Classic, which pitted two two-member teams against one another for hefty prize money. The series has run ten years and given away over $2,000,000.

In the early days of the Classic, Cary "The Dentist" Middlecoff, announcing in his drill-side manner and quiet southern drawl, lulled the viewer to sleep. Another announcer, also an expert commentator, was Tommy "The Grip" Armour, who most duffers remember vaguely as a near-great pro and more specifically as a foremost exponent of the golf grip as the way to solve most of their problems on the links.

In an effort to update the Classic with a more modern point of view, CBS replaced Middlecoff and Armour with Ken Venturi, a former U.S. Open champ and Ryder Cup player.

Middlecoff's homespun manner and Armour's tactical play-by-play gave way to Venturi's philosophical-implication approach. "Tensions run high," Venturi said of the Classic. "Sometimes you can hear it in the breathing of the golfers. That's when you know things are getting basic."

Despite the less-than-fascinating banter, the Classic was indeed a classic. It was one of the only team matches in existence, and the only one that paid off. The idea of partnership was attractive both to the golfers and the audience. Two against two put golf into the realm of a team sport. The long hitters would go for the birdie while the man with the short game would often play it safe for the par. Win or lose, the golfers were never alone.

Another plus was the fact that the sixteen matches were taped well in advance of air time. They were played in the fall and telecast on fifteen successive weeks during the winter. The main reason for this was editing: getting the best shots to the viewer, being able to assemble the pros during a three-week period rather than chasing them down week after week, which would have been the case had it been live; and taking out the "shits" and the "fucks," which the players were apt to scream when they blew a shot.

One major problem was with Jerry Heard, who had the habit of whistling into his microphone. It sounded like a spaceship shooting across the sky in one of those old sci-fi movies.

All the golfers were wired for sound—mikes around their necks and transmitters in their rear pockets. In this way, the audience got the real scoop from the players themselves. Furthermore, the matches were in color; stop-action was introduced (although it's been said that ABC's Roone Arledge really started that); and the pros were required to wear color-coordinated outfits, obey a stage manager who followed them around, and learn how to act in front of a camera. Things like getting out of the way.

Aside from the Classic, the only other major tournament covered by CBS is the Masters.

The Masters considers itself special. Old School, conservative, the Masters committee does not particularly like the hype and hyperbole delivered by ABC and NBC. The Masters chose CBS because the network does not cover the other three biggies—the U.S. and British Opens and the PGA. The Masters wants to be individualistic in all ways, right down to who covers it.

So much for the Columbia Broadcasting System, a gem in the world of television.

Ask anybody who knows anything about sports coverage, and they'll tell you that NBC is the best, not the biggest, but the best. From camera positions to commentary, NBC is supposed to be leagues ahead of the other networks.

In football, Curt Gowdy and Aldie Rogadis make their competition look like little kids by comparison. Before CBS wrested NBA coverage away from NBC and proceeded to lose half its audience, NBC wowed the fans with announcers who brought real passion, compassion, and knowledge to basketball commentary.

NBC's major problem, which CBS also shares, originates from upper-echelon planning. The two "killers," which made NBC synonomous with embarrassment, came about in the areas of football and the Winter Olympics in Japan. The network will probably never live them down.

When NBC's leaders negotiated for the Winter Olympics they forgot to include field positions for their commentators. When the network covered the games, Herb Geidy, a fine sportscaster, was in a studio with skier Billy Kidd and figure skater Peggy Flemming, all talking about what *had* happened on the slopes and in the rink. No cameras were placed at the starting and finishing lines. There was no spontaneity, the story line was lost.

The worst faux pas, already written in the annals of bad news, was "The Heidi Case."

The New York Jets had apparently won over the Oakland

Raiders. There were just minutes to go, so the network brass decided to cut away to *Heidi,* the first scheduled prime-time telecast of the night. *Heidi* began and so did Oakland. They scored twice and won the game. Someone reported seeing a guillotine being wheeled into NBC headquarters that night.

In 1973 NBC negotiated for and got two winter tournaments which, since their inception, have been among the most popular. The Dean Martin Tucson Open and the Bob Hope Desert Classic are lovely to look at, they pull the top pros, and pay off over $300,000 in prize money. NBC had previously done the Hawaiian and Andy Williams tournaments (both grabbed away by ABC) and the Crosby (also switched to ABC).

The chief commentators, Pat Hernon, Jay Randolph, and Jim Simpson, are all competent, with more excitement than the CBSers, but without the diversity and big-name personalities of ABC.

NBC sits halfway between the other two networks in personality broadcasting. The thinking runs along the same lines as it does at CBS—ABC has a lock on golf. In quantity, not particularly quality. It's a moot point.

Let's face it, ABC is the sportscasting giant in the television world. The network pulls all stops in its desire to puff up the sports event by throwing every conceivable personality into the picture.

We know about Howard Cosell, the voice of the distraught, downtrodden athlete. Jim Kelly, who broadcasts thirty-nine tournaments a year over NBC Monitor, says Cosell "is a frustrated actor. He just enjoys getting out and rapping with the coaches and players. He may be offensive to some, but nobody knows more than Howard in most areas."

Cosell does not show up for golf tournaments for two good reasons: the sport is not controversial enough, although during the last few years, what with the PGA court battles and national exposure, he'd be able to find some dirt; furthermore he has already had too much exposure on other telecasts. ABC feels that if Cosell were broadcasting tournaments much of the audience would be irritated. "What does *he* know about the game?" they would ask.

Cosell would also upset the balance ABC has in golf coverage where the idea of family prevails.

At the '73 PGA, ABC brought in its big guns. Regulars Davy Marr and Byron Nelson were the experts, Jim McKay was hauled away from Wide World of Sports, Frank Gifford had some time before football season began, Bill Flemming came on, and Chris Schenkel anchored.

I was standing with Terry Jastrow and his assistant on the practice green at Canterbury. We were talking about the commentators, what the ABC official view of them was, why they were chosen in the first place.

Terry, a medium-height blond who played golf with Homero Blancas and others down at the University of Houston, where good golfers are nurtured into great ones, put his articulate, slightly southern voice into gear.

"Basically, Chris Schenkel is the host of the show. I mean, if you ever had a situation, and I don't care what it is, where you wanted a guy to host the Olympics, or host the number-one NFL football game of the week, or the U.S. Open Championship, or a cocktail party at your own house, Chris Schenkel would be that guy.

"He's got a fantastic way with people, and an uncanny ability to block out every other thing on hand to pay attention to the topic he's immediately concerned with. In other words, is he were in a discussion with you right now, and there were 14,000 people going by and bugging him, he would still pay attention to only you.

"He's not like other guys, who carry on 3.5 conversations with a half dozen people all at once."

I told him Schenkel sometimes reminded me of a little kid who just lost his baseball cards and is trying like mad, in a nice way, to get them back from you.

He laughed and went on to Jim McKay: "The finest storyteller in all of sports. He has the ability to bring out the humanistic characteristics of the sport like no other man I've ever seen. It's not a guy with a one hundred-fifty-yard shot, but a man who's a shot behind, who has two children, maybe a young player on the tour."

Golf is one of the most humbling of all sports. It's great to see presidents or kings or very wealthy men shank a shot. When one of these people misses a shot all his medals and positions and wealth are stripped away, and he becomes just another person who trickled his ball into the rough. What McKay does is similar to this. He looks at the pro, builds a story around both his game and his life outside the course, making him not the great pro who never misses, but a person who happened to miss.

What about Frank Gifford, old Giff, Mr. Straight, whose velvet Scarsdale voice calls the play-by-play on Monday Night Football? And what's he doing at the PGA?

"Well," Terry was thinking, "he adds an identifiable nature to the telecast. People know Frank Gifford. His is a common name."

Gifford was sitting alone in one of the patio restaurants off the practice green, big black sunglasses, square jaw, gazing out over the course. A waitress stood beside him, waiting to serve.

The rationale behind having Giff in there is that he's interesting, attractive, a personality. Much better, according to Jastrow, then having nine boring golf experts.

"If there are things that Frank Gifford doesn't know about the game, there's always Byron Nelson and Dave Marr to pick up the slack."

Byron Nelson's Texas twang is as recognizable as Giff's face. So is Nelson's game. ABC never lets you forget that in 1945 Byron won eleven tournaments in a row and eighteen for the year. Credentials. He also loosens up the broadcast, just as Dandy Don Meredith does on Monday nights. A kind of chatty, lemme-tell' yuh-bout-it rap that offsets the straightforward tack used by the announcers out on the course.

Having Dave Marr in there is a good idea, especially at the PGA. Marr played in the tournament. When the pros came up to a hole, Marr had intimate knowledge of it, since just a few hours before he played the hole himself.

"Marr was voted Most Improved Golf Announcer last year," Terry told me.

"Yeah, by who?"

"The difference is amazing; he's come a long way."

"Who voted him Most Improved?"

"The way he analyzes is incredible; he has the ability to interject some very cogent, logical intricacies into the game of golf."

"Uh huh, but who. . . ?"

"I think you'll find him far more entertaining than articulate."

"No doubt. Listen, could you answer one question for me?"

"Shoot."

"Who voted Marr Most Improved? Just for the record."

"And I'm sure he'll continue to be that way. I'm very, very happy with Dave Marr, just as everyone at ABC is."

"ABC voted him Most Improved?"

"Then there's Bill Flemming."

Bill Flemming, right.

The single, greatest, number-one talk artist in the industry, that's what the network thinks of Bill Flemming. Which should make Cosell happy to know. "And by that," said Jastrow, "I mean he very rarely, if ever, fucks a word. In the heat of the live situation you'll get them every so often, you know they'll fuck them. Not Bill."

Wednesday afternoon.

With three days to go before air time, the operation has to be set up. Most announcers arrive on Wednesday. Some don't show up until Saturday morning. It's easy to tell who *they* are—they haven't done their homework. When they get on the air there are long pauses, incorrect information, no information at all.

Wednesday is a good time to arrive for another reason—

parties. Wednesday is Pro-Am day. After the round the pros and amateurs are ready for booze and food. The sports equipment companies are there, contacts are made. The pros with early tee times the next day usually leave early.

Thursday, for the television industry, is acclimation day. Monitors and cameras are checked for placement.

Friday is rehearsal day, getting the bugs out. The producer and director show the announcers what the nature of the coverage will be, the story line, and the communication lines from the towers to the booth are hooked up. The announcers, with the help of spotters, are told what to look for in certain golfers. By Friday night the leaders are in. Some of them might be unknowns.

A Chi Chi Rodriguez is easy to spot, but what about a Don Iverson? Is there a certain way he walks? What will he be wearing tomorrow? Something special probably, since he knows he'll be on national television.

On Saturday morning Byron Nelson records his Tip for Golfers. At the PGA it was different types of lies: flat, uphill, and downhill.

Time is getting short; they'll go on the air at 5:00. Everything has to be perfect. After all, this is one of the big ones for network.

3:15. The production people climb into the trailers and strap on their headsets.

3:30. The announcers make their trek to the towers. Ten holes will be covered for this one. The announcers pass early starters on their way to the locations. The leaders are far back, maybe just getting off on ten.

4:30. Chris Schenkel checks the mock-ups, small-scale models of the holes to be covered.

Back in 1970 there was a lot of flack from the viewers about the mock-ups. They were so unnatural, ran the argument. A blimp was used at the '71 PGA in Palm Beach, but the result was terrible. The blimp cameras flattened out the course, making it look like a blurry pie. The networks will have to live with the mock-ups until some genius on the production staff comes up with something better.

4:55. The lead in. Schenkel straightens out his tie and pulls his jacket down. Who buys his clothes for him? Flash Gordon? Byron Nelson's face looks like the roadmap of New Hampshire, Dave Marr looks very short.

"Welcome to the . . . " Schenkel begins.

More sports from TV land.

4
The Long Green: Supermoney

If an average guy, who also happened to be a top-notch golf pro, averaged even par last year on the tour, he would have pocketed anywhere between $90,000 and $110,000. Which, if he played his cards right, would have been peanuts compared to what he could have picked up *off* the course.

Thanks to TV, corporate finance, the sports manager, and the Superstar, the day of the big hitter–low collector are over. Golf is now in the big money, a game for the high rollers.

Until about ten years ago it was the amateur golfer with all the money. Playing out of an exclusive club, with expensive tastes and equipment, he and his cronies would play $1000 Nassaus or $25,000 Calcuttas. For them the game was an avocation, hardly ever an occupation. Who in his right mind could consider living on a few thousand bucks a year with no security and a chance that a bad streak might wipe him out?

Still, there were those who gave it a whack, even back in the dark ages when pro golf was mostly in the imaginary stage.

Back in 1934, for instance, Paul Runyan, a little guy who was good around the greens, went into extra holes against boomer Craig Wood to capture the PGA at Buffalo. Runyan went on to become the tour's leading money winner that year with $6767. That figure was good for fifth-place money in *one* tournament in 1973, when Nicklaus was top earner with over $300,000.

In 1972 Fred Marti, in 55th place, won $46,269, which, with the exception of Billy Casper's $63,000 in 1945, would have made Marti the leading money winner from 1934 until 1953.

In 1950 the total prize money was $459,950; in 1973 it rose above $8,000,000.

In 1946 the Tam O'Shanter wowed everyone with a purse of $45,000, extraordinary for that day. In 1972 the nod went to a foreign tournament—the Pacific Masters in Japan, which gave away $300,000, $65,000 of which went to winner Gay Brewer. Not to be outdone by the Japanese, who lay back for a hundred years before discovering the game in 1957, the World Open Golf Championship at Pinehurst CC in North Carolina offered an astronomical $500,000 for its two-week, eight-day fest.

It took Sam Snead thirty-five years to win a grand total of $775,000 on the tour. Lanny Wadkins, if things continue going his way, will be there soon. In two years on the tour he has earned more than $300,000.

As late as 1959, Art Wall led the pack with just over $50,000. Bobby Nichols picked that up in four days by winning the '73 Westchester Classic. Nichols has a penchant for winning big purses. He did it in the now-defunct $300,000 Dow Jones Open in 1971. Dow, and Alcan of Canada, have learned an expensive lesson: more research and less desire to be the biggest in a hurry should prevail. Both took a real bath and folded, Alcan after only one tournament.

Not only the money but the galleries as well have swelled over the years. The 1946 U.S. Open at Canterbury pulled in a paid attendance of just over 14,000 for the four days. At Pebble Beach in the '72 Open the crowd was *limited* to 80,000.

The reasons behind this upsurge in the golf world need a graph covering half the wall of Madison Square Garden—little blue, red, yellow, and green lines starting from the floor and rising to the ceiling.

Surprisingly, the professional golf tour itself was neither the only nor the major factor in bringing golf out of the private club and into the public eye.

War was. World War II in particular. After the entire nation was fused together in a united effort for so many years, the soldiers came home and found, for economic and social reasons, that they had a lot of extra time on their hands. What to do?

Play golf?

Why not? It was all part of leisure living, didn't take too much out of you, was competitive, and while the wars called for unity of action, the game of golf called for the individual to make his own destiny.

Entrepreneurs saw a hot prospect in the game, even before the war, and set out to take it out of the profit doldrums and make it pay.

These men saw courses being built every day, equipment showing up in the marketplace, books coming out on the swing, the grip, the stance; these tips brought the American golf public closer to the game, closer to the pros who offered their advice. Unlike the other sports which were more spectator oriented, golf was for the average guy.

Who could play football like Grantland Rice, baseball like Peewee Reese? Nobody but the other pros themselves. Few could keep up with Ben Hogan in golf, but every once in a while the ordinary duffer could chip in from fifty yards, and even Ben Hogan couldn't do that all the time.

What was even more attractive about the game was that it didn't matter who you were on the course. When it got down to nitty-gritty, everyone was the same on the amateur level, whether it was the President of the United States or a pipe fitter from Duluth. Golf, in that sense, was a great equalizer.

The entrepreneurs also knew that if golf was to become a major sport they would have to put the big names under their wings and bring them up along with the game itself.

In those early days there were two or three good-looking amateur prospects who were ready to take the plunge into commercialism. Those who finally persuaded them to were the folks who make a smile worth a million—the managers.

The first marriage between the man and his manager was consummated in 1937 with Sam Snead and Fred Corcoran. Snead was a country boy who played in bare feet and whacked the ball three miles. His appeal came not only from his ability to win, but to be winning. He had grabbed the West Virginia Open and the state's PGA title in 1936, which convinced him to go after the big money on the regular tour.

He chose the Hershey Open, where he placed fifth. The Dunlop Company, who generally knew a good thing when they saw it, promptly signed him to play their ball and clubs, paying him $500 and free equipment.

Success must have thrown him a little off balance, because he didn't do so well in the next two tournaments—the Miami-Baltimore and Nassau Opens in Florida—but maybe it was those flat courses, which for a West Virginian was a whole different game.

The Oakland Open in Los Angeles, the first of the 1937 tour in January, made up for it. He won and was deluged by offers from both tournament and individual sponsors.

Fred Corcoran's game was promotion. In 1936, Corcoran, a staid Bostonian and consummate raconteur, left individual hustling and took over as PGA tournament chairman. No mean job.

What Corcoran walked into was a bunch of dull golfers hardly anyone had heard of, playing a game few understood much less cared about, and traveling across a country on the heels of the Depression. He was hired to make golf exciting and make it pay.

First, the sponsors. Most sponsors at the time came from the towns in which the tournaments were played. Corcoran won them over with what he used best—logic.

"Do you know what it means to have seventy-five to one hundred professional golfers come to your town?" he asked.

"Tell us," they answered.

At least they were listening. But he couldn't be sure. "The money they will spend alone in your town, on food, clothing, lodging, not to mention entertainment, will be twice what you put up in prizes."

"Can you guarantee it?"

"On my life." Freddie was flamboyant that way.

He knew one thing for sure: the sponsors first had to buy him before they'd go for his package.

The deals were made.

His second problem was the press. Specifically, how to get reporters more interested, or interested at all, since most of the stuff from their typewriters smacked of the same dullness infecting the players themselves.

Freddie made the game come alive with quips, anecdotes, one-liners—all of which the sportswriters, who also wanted to get closer to the front page in the sports section, gobbled up.

The results looked promising.

More coverage, larger galleries, contented sponsors, bigger purses. In the two years between 1936 and 1938 Corcoran upped the purse money from $100,000 to $160,000, a percentage hike which even today would be astounding.

Corcoran admits he had to overcome one major barrier to pull it off. The main character in the drama was Snead himself.

The Slammer had become such a hot property that Walter Hagen's old touring partner, Joe Kirkwood, made him a substantial offer to leave the tour and make an exhibition swing around the country. The money involved was substantially more than Snead could have made on the tour.

Corcoran was nervous. His main attraction was suddenly going to leave the tour. Freddie soon after signed Sammy to an agreement which stipulated that he would be Snead's sole representative for exhibitions, matches, and all other matters pertaining to golf.

Snead went on to win the Crosby Pro-Am, the St. Paul Open, the Miami and Nassau Opens, finished second in the U.S. Open, and finished out the year in third place with more than $10,000.

Personality became a real factor in the promotion of the game. Following Snead, Ben Hogan, Byron Nelson, and Jimmy Demaret emerged the game's stars.

In more recent times, with the management business engaged in a multimedia operation, an entrepreneur not exclusively from the golf ranks entered the scene. Mark McCormack, who handles Palmer, Player, and until recently Nicklaus, among others, is catholic in his approach to sports management. He represents Jean-Claude Killy, Rod Laver, John Havlicek, Bill Shoemaker, and loads of others.

Palmer was McCormack's first golf client, and television was the medium through which Arnie was promoted. McCormack says about his star: "Palmer expresses his emotions in a fashion that film can capture. The flight of the golf ball may not make for scintillating sport TV—television has never been particularly at ease with its golf coverage—but the expressionistic qualities of Palmer made, and still make, excellent TV. Because of him, and especially his dramatic wins in the 1960 Masters and U.S. Open, golf became a spectator sport of the masses. Frank Beard says he owes twenty-five cents of every dollar he has made to Arnold Palmer, and he may well be right."

Nicklaus has those same qualities. His legendary determination matches his facial expression. He plows through the golf field, charging like Palmer, but is actually, say the people who should know, a better all-around golfer than Arnie ever was.

In keeping with his nose-to-the-grindstone image is an impeccable reputation. A family man who first goes to his wife and children after a win, he is at the apex of the American Puritan ethic. Add to that his heroic dimensions—the Golden Bear attack-

ing the course with Nordic vigor—Jack Nicklaus, like Palmer before him, is the real Mr. America.

Nicklaus and Palmer were too busy winning tournaments to
handle the commercial offers pouring in. Mack was happy to
oblige them. In these rugged men of integrity, he saw the perfect
combination for bringing them more money off the course than
they were making on it.

They've both become millionaires many times over. Arnie, for
instance, with Arnold Palmer Enterprises, golf-equipment plants,
driving ranges, franchised laundries, and golf academies, where a
kid can go for a summer and learn the game, grosses close to
$600,000,000 a year. To oversee it all he flies in his own Lear jet and
takes occasional vacations at his own private 27-hole course in
Orlando, Florida.

The difference between the Palmer of old and Palmer as
corporate giant has as much to do with high finance as it has with
low golf rounds. In 1959, when Arnie was a fledgling, he was
offered $500 a year by Heinz to use his name in association with
their ketchup. Today, when Palmer is asked to play a round of VIP
golf with executives from large corporations, his fee is $12,500—for
the day.

As further testimony of the long green money game, also in
1959 Munsingwear gave Palmer free shirts to wear while playing
on the tour. Today, he wears his own brand.

When it comes to money the competition factor figures off the
course often as much as it does on. In 1971 Palmer's major competitor through the years, Jack Nicklaus, broke away from
McCormack, deciding he could handle his own money matters.

The reason? First, Nicklaus had to live in Palmer's shadow for
most of his professional life. When Arnie began winning fewer
tournaments in the late sixties and early seventies and Jack began
winning more, a conflict of interest grew. He was tired of being
number two, when with a different manager he could be number
one, which he thought he should be, and rightly so.

The problem for McCormack and Nicklaus was having two
superstars with similar images. Either one of them could have fit

easily into any product endorsement or speaking engagement, and instead of a bidding situation (which would have happened if Nicklaus were with someone else), McCormack too often picked the man he had been with longer. To Nicklaus' consternation, Palmer usually got the nod.

Some people warned Nicklaus against going with Mack as his manager for just this reason. Though Jack and Arnie are different from one another in many ways, they have enough in common that endorsements can be laid on either one. This problem does not occur with two others in McCormack's stable: Gary Player and Lee Trevino.

Player became almost immediately recognizable the moment he hit the tour. His black-and-white outfits made him a landmark on the links. Player's salt-and-pepper march down the fairway gave the fans a new hero and the sportscasters a flashy new player to key on.

One thing that separates Player from Jack and Arnie is his size—5′8″ and 159 pounds. Diminutive, without the burly, go-getem of the others. He showed the television viewers that—yes—a little guy can play ball with the big fellas. In order to do this he developed his body to a point where he could say, "I haven't one ounce of fat on me."

His exercising was one of the best advertisements for getting the body together. The smaller golfers of the world saw in Player an answer to their frustrations and an end to the cliché which said that a good big man can always beat a good small man.

Vitamin-pill manufacturers and health-food outfits would have been naturals to get Player to endorse their products, but none has come up with enough money.

Player has other ties: the South African Marine Shipping Corporation (which agrees to ship his horses for nothing), South African Airways, Coca-Cola, and Ford of South Africa. His other interests include a golf-course architecture company that is building clubs in South Africa and Rhodesia, the Edblow mattress company, and Jungle Oats cereal, among others.

Some of the first people who chase after a hot or potentially hot golfer are the golf-equipment manufacturers. It's a sticky business for the pro who has signed with a ball or club manufacturer and suddenly discovers that his game is going to hell as a result of it.

McCormack tells how Player, in 1961, had two offers from the equipment men, one from First Flight, the other from Shakespeare:

"The president of First Flight was a man named Jack Harkins, a flamboyant personality well-known on the golf tour for his antic behavior. He enjoyed, for example, trying to pay dinner checks with a $1000 bill he always carried. . . . Gary got on well enough with First Flight, but a few years later, shortly bafore his First Flight contract was due to expire, we got a call from the Shakespeare Company, primarily a manufacturer of fiberglass fishing rods. Shakespeare wanted to make a major impact on the golf-club market with fiberglass shafts. The company felt that to do this properly it had to have the endorsement of one of the Big Three—Palmer, Player, or Nicklaus. By now Palmer had his own club manufacturing company and Nicklaus had signed an excellent long-term contract with MacGregor, so Player was Shakespeare's only hope."

After Player swung the clubs for a few weeks—and liked them okay—Mack and Gary agreed to meet with Shakespeare in Dallas, and out of fairness to First Flight they invited Jack Harkins along with his own case.

The four of them met in the room. Harkins brought along some First Flight clubs and some Shakespeare as well. One of the first things Harkins did was accuse the fiberglass shafts of not being strong enough to endure the power of the pro tour (which was later proved).

"All of a sudden he stood up," McCormack recalled, "and said in his boisterous way, 'These clubs have so much torque you can twist the heads right off them.' Harkins was a strong man, and he picked up one of the Shakespeare clubs, took the grip in his left hand and the head in his right and sure enough, he twisted the head until it just about fell off the shaft. Well, that was more than Henry Shakespeare could bear. Henry jumped up and said, 'You can take First Flight irons and you can bend them right over your knee like nothing,' and he picked up one of Harkin's irons and bent it into an L, just like he said. So Jack twisted off another head, just to show how effortlessly he could do it, and Henry bent another iron, and pretty soon the argument was down to who could break the other guy's golf clubs using the least possible effort, and there were ruined golf clubs everywhere. As far as we were concerned Henry won the argument—with his money, not his clubs—and Player signed with Shakespeare."

Player later had a lot of trouble with the fiberglass shafts, and started using another brand. Shakespeare bugged him so much that he went out and painted his other clubs in that same off-gray color used on the fiberglass shafts. Shakespeare got tougher and Player finally said he'd use them. He did and won the 1965 U.S. Open. "To this day," says McCormack, "Player considers that to be his greatest golfing achievement—simply because he won with glass shafts."

Both Mack and Player figured that a win at the Open was repayment enough for Henry Shakespeare, and the contract was quickly terminated.

Player's smallness and eccentricity are not the only reasons why he's such a promotable man. A number of pros have those characteristics. Player is also a big drawing card for his golf. He holds the distinction, along with Gene Sarazen, Ben Hogan, and Nicklaus, of having won the four major titles. He took the U.S. Open in 1965, the British Open in 1959 and 1968, the PGA in 1962 and 1972 and the Masters in 1961. His career winnings are well past the million-dollar mark.

The Black Knight, as a newsman once dubbed him, is also the perfect gentleman, on a par with any diplomat. He seldom gets angry, and when he does he never shows it. Discipline and endurance, which have brought him to the top of the golf world, have also given him the control to remain there.

In the game of promotion and big money, another of Mack's boys makes waves whether he wins or loses. Lee Trevino's story is a classic example of the rags-to-riches romance, for which Sam Snead is so famous.

In the spring of 1967, so the story goes, Lee's wife sent in the $20 entry fee to the U.S. Open in Baltusrol, a fee they could hardly afford. "I had a round-trip airline ticket and a grand total of $450 between me and the goal post," Trevino said. He got hot in a hurry and wound up in fifth place with a healthy check for $6000.

Though he was born in Dallas, most people think, due to the publicity, that he somehow escaped over the Mexican border with a three iron in his hands and went on to show WASPs everywhere that a "wetback" could drive and chip his way into golfdom.

In seven years on the tour he's won over $1,000,000, and in his heyday, 1971, even though he finished second behind Nicklaus by about $13,000, he was named Golfer of the Year by the PGA, Male Athlete of the Year by the Associated Press, and Sportsman of the Year by *Sports Illustrated.*

He accomplished it all with his game and his mouth. A perpetual rapper, Trevino cracks jokes (most of them funny), offers opinion on everything from Baked Alaska to Texas Mud. The aspirin company that signed him to do commercials probably had his audience in mind. "They're more prone to get headaches listening to him," said one pro who Trevino bothers on the course with his talking, "than Lee is talking at them."

With Palmer, Player, and Trevino in the stable Mack doesn't need much more. He is at the head of the family of golf managers. Close behind McCormack is another top manager, Ed Barner, president of Uni-Managers International out of Los Angeles.

Barner is a close personal friend of Billy Casper's, whom he handles, along with Bruce Crampton, Chi Chi Rodriguez, Johnny Miller, and others. Barner has turned Casper's $1,300,000 earnings into ten to fifteen times that. He has also promoted Casper in a role at which Gary Player excels—golf ambassadorships.

Casper, a Mormon Church member who quotes the Bible when asked questions by the press, is an easy-going guy. He's calmed down considerably since the early days back in 1954 when he first hit the tour, fat and jolly at one moment and off in heavy depression the next. The most unusual thing about Casper had to do with that fat, and how he got rid of it. He shaved off forty pounds in 1965 by eating things like buffalo meat, ground bear in green peppers, and reindeer stew.

Not much there for Barner to work with.

Even on the course he doesn't sparkle like the others; while the leaders are battling for position, from out of the rear, bouncing along the fairway is Little Billy, making a shambles out of par. At the 1973 Sammy Davis in Hartford, the 35,000 gallery members had their eyes on Lee Elder, who if he won would finally get to the Masters as the first black, Palmer, who was mounting one of his charges, and Lee Trevino, grabbing their attention with jokes.

While all the hoopla was going on, Casper held in his stomach and squeezed through for the victory.

"Casper!" someone exclaimed. "Where'd *he* come from?"

Casper called it. Earlier in the day he said in his prophetic voice, "There's no chance for a playoff. Somebody's going to shoot it up around here and there won't be any need for any extra holes. It's that kind of a track. It'll be that kind of a day."

He forgot to mention that he would be the one to do it.

Even the other pros are surprised when he sneaks through. Here's Bruce Devlin: "I'm leading the tournament, shoot 66, and get beat. That's really something. How often does this kind of thing happen? I've never seen a tournament with such a bloody scramble in all my life. I just shot 265 for four days and I'm going to have to be satisfied with second-place money."

Because Casper's only apparent salable commodity is that he wins, Ed Barner had to find an outlet for his other talents, whatever they were.

An ambassador of golf, thought Barner, why not? He makes enough on the tour and by endorsing a life-insurance company, hair tonic, a golf-equipment company, a clothing manufacturer, and a franchising operation.

Whenever there's a championship in a foreign country—

Japan is the most popular for the money it offers American pros—
Casper is sent out. Like a top-notch foreign service officer, he is
always congenial. His discipline on the course carries over to
meeting with heads of foreign countries.

Johnny Miller is a whole other matter. It's been said (and
proven) that any man who wins one of the Big Four during any
given year can expect to make more than a million dollars from it.
Miller is a prime example.

The year before he won the U.S. Open in 1973, he was voted
the Best Dressed Golfer. A natural for Sears to sign him for an
estimated $200,000 to wear their clothes on national television.

"He may look a little stiff," said a Sears official, "with that
wave he gives on the commercials. Let's face it, he's not an actor.
But he wears clothes very well."

I asked him what he thought about Miller accusing the PGA
of "tricking up the greens" at the PGA Championship. Were potential buyers put off by it?

"Hell no, sales went up."

Of all his clients, Barner says, Miller has the best shot at
gathering in the most money. Miller, at twenty-six, is a member of
the "Mod Squad," the group of young golfers who are out to
dethrone the big boys, Nicklaus, Player, Trevino and Casper.
Along with Lanny Wadkins, Grier Jones, Jerry Heard, and rookie
Ben Crenshaw, Miller has cut a wedge into both tour winnings and
commercial endorsements.

Speaking of Gentle Ben Crenshaw. At twenty-one, he's the
most sought-after and popular rookie to hit the tour since Palmer
and Nicklaus.

Crenshaw's flirtation with managers began a few years ago
with Vinny Giles, rated by *Golf Digest* as 1972's number two amateur. Giles himself turned pro, not as a golfer but a manager.

His first two clients were Allen Miller and Bob Dickson.
Miller, like Giles, played golf at the University of Georgia, and
Dickson beat Giles by one·stroke in the 1967 U.S. Amateur. But
what Giles really needed to make his new operation go was a

superstar. He went after Crenshaw, about whom John Schlee, another young pro, said, "Crenshaw *draws* people. You send him out in the middle of a desert with a sand wedge and all of a sudden there'd be 10,000 fans."

"Crenshaw is a handsome kid," said Giles, "a nice young man with great ability. Girls like him. TV likes him. And he'll make a bundle before he ever tees it up in his first major tournament.

"He has more going for him than any golfer in history. More than Palmer and, yes, even more than Nicklaus. Jack makes millions as a commercial figure now, but it was tough selling that fat, short-haired kid from Ohio ten years ago."

Giles didn't get Crenshaw. Neither did McCormack, who thought he had it in the bag. Giles, who at the time thought Crenshaw and Steve Melnyck had both gone with McCormack, said this about his own operation. "We take a fee based on our overhead. Then we take a percentage of the outside income we help to generate. Our fee can go no higher than $10,000 a year, no matter what the client makes."

McCormack, on the other hand, gets twenty percent of everything the pro makes, including tour winnings. Melnyck went for Mack's track record. Crenshaw shifted back and forth for a while and finally chose to go with his idol, Nicklaus, who, as soon as he broke from McCormack, set up Golden Bear, Inc.

"They just want me to go out and play golf the first year and not worry about anything," Crenshaw said. The only contract he's signed is with *Golf Magazine* as a member of its professional staff.

Of course there are those whom the long green has eluded. Promising rookies who after one year and no money on the tour go back home to work in the plant. Of the twenty-five members of the 1972 Tournament Players Division graduating class, only Tom Kite made enough to earn a year's exemption from qualifying. He placed 56th in money winnings with $54,270. At the bottom of the list was John Morgan, a Canadian, who finished 283d with $1167. Morgan and the other twenty-three who missed the cut will have to proceed directly to GO and begin all over again.

One interesting case involves a switch-over, a star in one sport who gave up his career to make a go at the tour. So far, Ken Harrelson, ex-Boston Red Sox superslugger, has struck out.

"The Hawk" gave up his $70,000-a-year bat for a $100,000 driver, but in both attempts to qualify in the TPD school he didn't make it. Bob Toski, who gave him tips and encouragement at the outset, is convinced that Harrelson will make it if "he can control his natural power and give the devotion demanded to play good golf."

He also has to control his temper. At the 1973 Atlanta Classic, one of the invitationals he could play in as a nonqualifier, he showed up at the first tee and was immediately slapped with a two-stroke penalty for being late. What happened was just like the old days when he blasted umpires—he went haywire at Atlanta, hitting the ball so poorly that he withdrew after eighteen. He said it took weeks to get over it, which is not the kind of discipline it takes to make it on tour, where the pros must immediately forget about a bad shot in order to place in the money.

The general feeling around the tour is that if the Hawk is going to make it, he is going to have to get hungry, eat some of that lettuce Tony Lema said all rabbits have to chew on before hitting the big time.

What Harrelson, the rookies, and the established pros are all after is the cash. Professional golf is funny that way—not that pros in other sports aren't after it too—but when we look at final statistics in golf, it's always what place on the money list the man falls that is most important. In other sports it may be a batting average, yards gained, field-goal percentage; the money aspect is more hidden from the public. In golf, every week, right there on the front page, is the List. How many people ever look at a golfer's scoring average or performance average, PGA exemption-point standings or average money per tour event? Few that I know of, except the pros themselves.

When we look at the history of golf we see the greats like Sarazen, Snead, Hogan, and the rest of them, but we can't quite remember who won what, when or how many times. Or if they won it at all.

It has to do with the nature of the game itself. Jack Nicklaus has been the leading money winner six of the last ten years. A valuable statistic, but how did he do it? What about some of those great finishes? In golf great finishes are a dime a dozen. Every week someone rams through to nab the top money. Arnold Palmer's classic charges. On the back nine, seven down with five holes to go, he begins—birdie, par, birdie, birdie, eagle. Where was that, and who did he squeeze by for the victory?

Golf has been accused of being the most unexciting of all sports—to watch. It's also been said that the very idea of one man being able to win over $300,000 a year is the most electric thing about the game. At the beginning of each year the slate is wiped clean; every pro starts at zero and has to rely on his ability alone to survive. No salaries are paid, and if a guy has a bad year he takes a dive. In other sports if he's off, his salary is reduced the next time around.

For that single reason above all others—that the golf professional cannot live on past performance, that he must begin to build from day one—makes golf THE money game.

The Stats

Since World War II over $75,000,000 in prize money has been given to the pros, but to show how tough the game is, more than half that—over $46,000,000—has been grabbed by only one hundred men. And only five of those—Jack Nicklaus, Arnold Palmer, Bill Casper, Lee Trevino, and Bruce Crampton—have become millionaires in "official" money earnings, which means that the tournaments have been sanctioned by official groups like the PGA and USGA.

The fact that Sam Snead is the all-time tournament winner, for instance, with 84 since 1937, doesn't mean he's won the most money. Jack Nicklaus has with only 51 victories. Snead is in 25th place with $563,752; Nicklaus, through 1973, has amassed $2,012,067. Ben Hogan, with 62 tour victories since 1938, is not in the top fifty. Bruce Crampton, with 14 wins since 1957, has won $1,065,709.

All of which shows two important things: the price of golf has gone up in recent years; and to win is often not as important as being consistent. Crampton is consistent, so is Bobby Nichols, who has won fewer than 10 times but has picked up almost $750,000.

America has been, and probably always will be statistic crazy, which makes it easy to make comparisons between past and present performances.

Money winnings took a noticable jump after World War II. Ben Hogan nabbed the honors in 1941 and 1942 with $18,358 and $13,143 respectively. Byron Nelson won in 1944 with $37,967 and 1945 with $63,335. War-bond prizes were awarded in 1943.

Past Money Winners (1946–1958)

Year	Player	Money
1946	Ben Hogan	$42,556
1947	Jimmy Demaret	27,936
1948	Ben Hogan	32,112
1949	Sam Snead	31,593
1950	Sam Snead	35,758
1951	Lloyd Mangrum	26,088
1952	Julius Boros	37,032
1953	Lew Worsham	34,002
1954	Bob Toski	65,819
1955	Julius Boros	63,121
1956	Ted Kroll	72,835
1957	Dick Mayer	65,835
1958	Arnold Palmer	42,607

1959

Player	Money
1. Art Wall	$53,167
2. Gene Littler	38,296
3. Dow Finsterwald	33,906
4. Bill Casper	33,899
5. Arnold Palmer	32,461
6. Mike Souchak	31,807
7. Bob Rosburg	31,676
8. Doug Ford	31,009
9. Jay Herbert	26,034
10. Ken Venturi	25,886

1960

Player	Money
1. Arnold Palmer	$75,262
2. Ken Venturi	41,230
3. Dow Finsterwald	38,541
4. Bill Casper	31,060
5. Jay Hebert	29,748
6. Mike Souchak	28,903
7. Doug Ford	28,411
8. Gene Littler	26,837
9. Bill Collins	26,496
10. Doug Sanders	26,470

1961

Player	Money
1. Gary Player	$64,450
2. Arnold Palmer	61,191
3. Doug Sanders	57,428
4. Bill Casper	37,776
5. Jay Hebert	35,583
6. Johnny Pott	32,267
7. Gay Brewer	31,149
8. Bob Goalby	30,918
9. Gene Littler	29,245
10. Billy Maxwell	28,335

1962

Player	Money
1. Arnold Palmer	$81,448
2. Gene Littler	66,200
3. Jack Nicklaus	61,868
4. Bill Casper	61,842
5. Bob Goalby	46,240
6. Gary Player	45,838
7. Doug Sanders	43,385
8. Dave Ragan	37,327
9. Bobby Nichols	34,311
10. Dow Finsterwald	33,619

1963

Player	Money
1. Arnold Palmer	$128,230
2. Jack Nicklaus	100,040
3. Julius Boros	77,356
4. Tony Lema	67,112
5. Gary Player	55,455
6. Dow Finsterwald	49,862
7. Mason Rudolph	39,120
8. Al Geiberger	34,126
9. Don January	33,754
10. Bobby Nichols	33,604

1964

Player	Money
1. Jack Nicklaus	$113,284
2. Arnold Palmer	113,203
3. Bill Casper	90,653
4. Tony Lema	74,130
5. Bobby Nichols	74,012
6. Ken Venturi	62,465
7. Gary Player	61,449
8. Mason Rudolph	52,568
9. Juan Rodriguez	48,338
10. Mike Souchak	39,559

1965

Player	Money
1. Jack Nicklaus	$140,752
2. Tony Lema	101,816
3. Bill Casper	99,931
4. Doug Sanders	72,182
5. Gary Player	69,964
6. Bruce Devlin	67,657
7. Dave Marr	63,375
8. Al Geiberger	59,699
9. Gene Littler	58,898
10. Arnold Palmer	57,770

1966

Player	Money
1. Bill Casper	$121,944
2. Jack Nicklaus	111,419
3. Arnold Palmer	110,467
4. Doug Sanders	80,096
5. Gay Brewer	75,687
6. Phil Rogers	68,360
7. Gene Littler	68,345
8. R. H. Sikes	67,348
9. Frank Beard	66,041
10. Al Geiberger	63,220

1967

Player	Money
1. Jack Nicklaus	$188,988
2. Arnold Palmer	184,065
3. Bill Casper	129,423
4. Julius Boros	126,785
5. Dan Sikes	111,508
6. Doug Sanders	109,455
7. Frank Beard	105,778
8. George Archer	84,344
9. Gay Brewer	78,548
10. Bob Goalby	77,106

1968

Player	Money
1. Bill Casper	$205,168
2. Jack Nicklaus	155,285
3. Tom Weiskopf	152,946
4. George Archer	150,972
5. Julius Boros	148,310
6. Lee Trevino	132,127
7. Arnold Palmer	114,602
8. Dan Sikes	108,330
9. Miller Barber	105,845
10. Bob Murphy	105,595

1969

Player	Money
1. Frank Beard	$175,223
2. Dave Hill	156,423
3. Jack Nicklaus	140,167
4. Gary Player	123,897
5. Bruce Crampton	118,955
6. Gene Littler	112,737
7. Lee Trevino	112,417
8. Ray Floyd	109,956
9. Arnold Palmer	105,128
10. Bill Casper	104,689

1970

Player	Money
1. Lee Trevino	$157,037
2. Bill Casper	147,372
3. Bruce Crampton	142,609
4. Jack Nicklaus	142,148
5. Arnold Palmer	128,853
6. Frank Beard	124,690
7. Dick Lotz	124,539
8. Larry Hinson	120,897
9. Bob Murphy	120,639
10. Dave Hill	118,415

1971

Player	Money
1. Jack Nicklaus	$244,490
2. Lee Trevino	231,202
3. Arnold Palmer	209,603
4. George Archer	147,769
5. Gary Player	120,916
6. Miller Barber	117,359
7. Jerry Heard	112,389
8. Frank Beard	112,337
9. Dave Eichelberger	108,312
10. Bill Casper	107,276

1972

Player	Money
1. Jack Nicklaus	$320,542
2. Lee Trevino	214,805
3. George Archer	145,027
4. Grier Jones	140,177
5. Jerry Heard	137,198
6. Tom Weiskopf	129,422
7. Gary Player	120,719
8. Bruce Devlin	119,768
9. Tommy Aaron	118,924
10. Lanny Wadkins	116,616

1973

Player	Money
1. Jack Nicklaus	$308,362
2. Bruce Crampton	274,266
3. Tom Weiskopf	245,463
4. Lee Trevino	210,017
5. Lanny Wadkins	200,455
6. Miller Barber	184,014
7. Hale Irwin	130,388
8. Billy Casper	129,474
9. John Miller	127,833
10. John Schlee	118,017

All-Time Money Leaders

Player	Money
1. Jack Nicklaus	$2,012,067
2. Arnold Palmer	1,643,651
3. Bill Casper	1,421,502
4. Lee Trevino	1,069,440
5. Bruce Crampton	1,065,709
6. Gary Player	984,349
7. Julius Boros	926,310
8. Gene Littler	921,275
9. Tom Weiskopf	884,639
10. Frank Beard	879,519
11. Miller Barber	827,343
12. George Archer	787,188

Player	Money
13. Doug Sanders	760,937
14. Bobby Nichols	741,211
15. Dave Hill	718,378
16. Dan Sikes	716,437
17. Tommy Aaron	691,660
18. Gay Brewer	656,180
19. Bob Goalby	609,383
20. Bruce Devlin	598,729
21. Dave Stockton	592,925
22. Bert Yancey	589,807
23. Don January	586,371
24. Juan Rodriguez	583,320
25. Sam Snead	563,752

Tournament Prize Money

Year	Events	Total Purses	Average Purse
1945	36	$ 435,380	$ 12,094
1946	37	411,533	11,123
1947	31	352,500	11,371
1948	34	427,000	12,559
1949	25	338,200	13,528
1950	33	459,950	13,938
1951	30	460,200	15,340
1952	32	498,016	15,563
1953	32	562,704	17,585
1954	26	600,819	23,108
1955	36	782,010	21,723

Year	Events	Total Purses	Average Purse
1956	36	847,070	23,530
1957	32	820,360	25,636
1958	39	1,005,800	25,789
1959	43	1,102,474	25,639
1960	41	1,187,340	28,959
1961	45	1,461,830	32,485
1962	49	1,790,320	36,537
1963	43	2,044,900	47,497
1964	41	2,301,063	56,123
1965	36	2,848,515	79,403
1966	36	3,074,445	85,401
1967	37	3,979,162	108,356
1968	45	5,077,600	112,835
1969	47	5,465,875	116,295
1970	47	6,259,501	133,181
1971	52	6,587,976	126,689
1972	46	6,954,649	151,188
1973	47	8,657,225	184,196

Take a Little—Give a Little

Back in 1962 Gary Player promised that if he ever won the U.S. Open he would donate his money to charity. Three years later, in St. Louis, after 72 holes two foreigners had tied for the lead. Player and Australian Kel Nagle entered extra holes.

Sudden death—for which we can thank TV, as it later ruined golf's head-to-head battle—had not yet been introduced, so Player and Nagle had to play another 18. Player won 71-74. Nagle got flustered, hitting two spectators along the way.

At the presentation ceremony Player donated $5000 of his $25,000 to cancer research and the other $20,000 to the USGA to help promote junior golf.

Player's gesture made it known to the viewing audience that golf's money game was not played simply as another way to rack up dollars for one's self.

Of all major sports, golf is the leader in charity. The real leading money winners on the tour never have to sink a putt. After the players have collected their checks, the clubs are paid off, and the help is taken care of, dozens of local and national charities take in the rest. During the last eight years these organizations have been given over $5,000,000.

Some of the bigs ones include:

The Bob Hope Desert Classic—over $1,000,000 in ten years for the Eisenhower Clinic.

The Western Open—over $350,000 in eight years for Evans Foundation caddie scholarships.

Houston Invitational—$169,000 in twenty years for scholarships and local youth golf programs.

Los Angeles Open—$150,000 in ten years for local community projects.

Sahara Invitational—$120,000 for four years for the United Fund.

Doral Open—$108,000 in one year to the Cancer Society.

National Golf Day—$1,500,000 in twenty years for education and research in golf-related organizations.

Westchester Classic—$1,800,000 since 1967 for the United Hospitals of Westchester County.

Two years ago the Westchester Classic was known as the "world's richest tournament" for putting up $250,000 in prize money.

The Westchester Country Club in Harrison, New York, is the kind of place—old-school opulence—that would bring in a lot of money just by the way it looks, and because the people who play there are some of the wealthiest in the country.

Barbara Haines, press chairman for the '73 Classic, is one of the volunteers, known as Twigs, who put it all together for the United Hospitals. She was the first Twig at the door when I walked in.

"The trouble with being known as the world's richest," she told me, "was that potential donors figured the Classic didn't need their money if it was so well off. When Jackie Gleason's Inverarry Classic came up with a bigger purse, we all breathed a sigh of relief and quickly became the "world's most charitable tournament.'"

"What kind of promotion do you do?"

"Oh, you know," she smiled. "Bank mailing, department-store displays, and an awful lot of things from Eastern Airlines—like six-foot replicas of Jack Nicklaus, bumper stickers."

Other Twigs started milling around. All charming. And I just knew from the way they spoke without moving their lips that somewhere in their lives was a Radcliffe, a Smith College, maybe even a Bennington.

"Then we have the grand patrons who give like $5000. Patrons give $1200. I think we have about twenty-five grand patrons. You could figure out your math."

"That's . . . "

"Right, and then we raffle off a car, a Mercedes or a Cadillac, wherever we can get the best deal. White Plains Ford is popular at the moment."

"What about the club itself, what kind of percentage does it get?"

"Oh, somewhere around $100,000 for expenses; the hospital gets the rest. I don't think the club made much last year."

"How come?"

"Well, you know, this is a charity operation, and normally expenses that the club incurs are probably as much as they get back. I mean, they don't, it's not the something they just *take*. I'm sure they . . . I don't know."

So much for that.

Though the Westchester Classic is no small potato, the big

drawing cards in the charity race are the celebrity tournaments, expecially the west-coasters at the beginning of each year: The Bing Crosby Pro-Am (January 3–6), Dean Martin Tucson Open (January 17–20), Andy Williams San Diego Open (January 24–27), Bob Hope Desert Classic (February 6–10) and the Glen Campbell Los Angeles Open (February 14–17).

In 1937 and 1938 Snead won the Crosby event and provided one of the high humor points of the '38 tour year.

Bing walked over to Sam and gave him his first-place check.

"If you don't mind, Mr. Crosby," said the suspicious Snead, "I'd rather have cash." The check was for $2500. Thirty-six years later in the 1974 Crosby the winner's share was $37,000.

During the war a different kind of charity was in action. Crosby and Hope put on exhibitions and matches in order to sell war bonds. Which they did by the millions.

Crosby has given over $2,000,000 to charity over the years, mostly to Bing Crosby's Youth Fund, loans for needy students at seventy-two small colleges and universities.

Bob Hope, who stayed away from celebrity golf for nearly twenty-five years, was persuaded in 1960 to have his name attached to the Palm Springs tournament. It was charity that made him do it. Of the $2,500,000 he's already contributed, the Eisenhower Medical Center has received well over half.

Hope doesn't need grand patrons to foot the bill: last year 432 amateurs paid $1500 apiece to play, and the list is growing. At the Crosby one year a man offered to pay $20,000 in hard cash to play. He was turned down, since the list is selective.

There are numerous reasons why amateurs want to play in these tournaments. One is that they look like floor shows at Caesar's Palace: buxom Twinkies parading around, an all-star cast, the weather, and the fact that Hope, Crosby, and company are all low-handicap golfers—all, that is, except Sammy Davis, Jr., who wasn't seen very much at the 1973 Sammy Davis Hartford Open. But then golf is not one of his games.

Charity golf is a two-way street: the charities feed the sport and vice versa. And even when the money derived from tournament does not go directly to a golf-related activity, the publicity itself and the help it brings are always on the plus side.

Nicklaus Plus Two for a Million

No mention of golf's long green money game is complete without an activity related to all sports—gambling. The amateur may bet anything from a dollar Nassau to $25,000 Calcuttas. The pros bet among themselves every once in a while, but more often put their money on other sports.

Every once in a while we see in the paper the odds on, say, Nicklaus, at 5-1 to win the Masters. Only a fool would bet on that. There are too many variations in golf, too many surprises, too many players. And since the game is played individual against individual the chances for an outside shot to slip into the winner's circle are too, too good. If for some weird reason people started betting heavily on golf tournaments, I'd become an instant bookie. And clean up.

Take the ordinary club hustler a la sociologist. He'll walk into the course, look around for a few guys who play to an 18 handicap but admit to a 12 because it makes them look better, and challenge them to a match. Nothing big. Maybe a $25 Nassau. This hustler is not on a one-shot deal; he wants to nurture the players, prime them for the big kill.

He'll go along if a player suggests upping it to $50 and play his game according to what he needs to make, no less, no more.

That was Don Petrie ten years ago, before he came to the conclusion that he could be a wealthy man if he made hustling a full-time job.

"I was making fifty, a hundred bucks on weekends and Wednesday afternoons. Big deal. I'm young then, wasn't married. Why not quit my job? So I did."

Petrie, thirty-six years old, short, he looks like an accountant, which eliminates the intimidation factor. "You gotta be stupid to walk up to the first tee looking like you're out to take them. I'm there for a friendly game for a few bucks."

Once, a long time ago, he wanted to be an actor. Actors need costumes. Petrie has them. "Basic ones. First of all, I'm a little guy, which helps. No little guy hits a long ball. Second, I go one or two ways with the clothes and the equipment. Sometimes I'm a shlub; there's nothing like a shirt with buttons on it to throw them off. Who wears buttons? And a hat. I like hats. I must have thirty, forty of them around the house. You know the kind: red with 'Happy Marsh CC' on the front. Brand-new shoes. Always. The ones you buy at Herman's in New York.

"Then the clubs. Another Herman's special. Arnold Palmer irons and Billy Casper woods. Nine irons, four woods, and a vinyl bag thrown in, all for a hundred ninety-five. But not new. That's important cause I can't go out looking like it's my first round. And shoot an 85? Forget it. I'd lose all the action."

Petrie started his career in southern Florida, where he returns every winter. His summers are spent on Long Island and in Westchester, but mostly at Bethpage on the island.

"You gotta understand one thing about Bethpage. With its five courses you don't run into the same people all the time, so your reputation doesn't get around. Besides, I have a good one. I never win by a lot and sometimes I lose to keep things on the up-and-up.

"Even when I hustle a new guy for a lot of money and beat him good, that kind of guy always wants to get his money back. So I gave him more strokes or he gives me less and I knock him off again. I remember one time I was playing the Black Course at Bethpage, which is the toughest. It's only around 6500 but plays seven. I like the Black. It's got the best action and unless your game is steady it'll rip you apart.

"Anyway, I was playing with these two guys from the garment district. It was on a Thursday afternoon, and I'd been sitting around the first tee, talking to the starter—the usual—and I hear these guys telling each other how good they are. Loud. I figured they must want everybody else to know too. So I get up and asked them if they need a third.

"They look at me, my hat, my skinny body, and I could read their mind easy. Here is a real fish, they're saying to themselves. All right, I can see they're pretty well off, they look expensive. It ought to be a good day.

"One of them, the big guy, says he plays to a 12 handicap, the other one's got a 16. Could be. Now I gotta make a decision. Am I gonna play a low ball with a little Nassau on the side or am I gonna take them both on, me against them. Golf matches are never won on the course, never, they're won on the tee, the first tee. On the Black Course I was playing to an eight, which meant if I played them both I'd split the difference—my eight to their eleven. I'd give them three strokes. They took it.

"I got worried. Were they hustling me? Then I got irritated. Irritated . . . I was pissed. Not only 'cause they might have been hustlers, but also I didn't like them. They acted like big shots, and I was some dummy they'd take for a ride.

"Sal, the big guy, wanted to know how much I wanted to play for. He hesitated and then came in with $10 a hole. He wanted ten like a hole in the head. His friend Sam helped the situation with automatic presses at ten apiece. Which meant if they were down by one at any time after the sixth hole a new bet would be made, starting even. I still had to give them strokes, if I owed them. They were smart about that. They took their three on the back nine, so if they started pressing on any hole from six to twelve they'd still get the three. I gave them one apiece on thirteen, fourteen, and seventeen.

"After the first hole, which Sal won with a par, he walked up to me and wanted to raise the ante."

"I waited long enough to make them think I was pondering the question and then said, sure, what to?"

" 'How 'bout fifty?' "

" 'Uh, lemme check,' " I said, pulling out my wallet and

turning away so they couldn't see how much I had. Eight hundred and change. 'It's a deal.'

"I won the third hole and after six we were still even. They won the seventh and I pressed. I won the eighth and ninth and they pressed.

"It didn't take long to figure they weren't hustlers, not pros anyway, but they thought they were. On every hole they huddled off the tee and planned their strategy. Sal, since he was bigger and longer off the tee, would go for the bird, while Sam, whose short game had to be better, would play it safe and go for the par. Before we teed off on the tenth Sal proposed a side bet, a five-hundred-dollar whip on the back side only.

"Normally I would have jumped at it, but I still owed them three strokes—I got them down to two—and they were lucky. Especially Sam. He didn't hit a long ball but he was steady. He also made a couple rebound shots on the front side—one off the rocks on three that left him five feet from the pin and a par, and an iron on seven that hit the flag and dropped two inches from the hole. Which I didn't need. Big Sal was off in the woods somewhere, and if it weren't for lucky Sam I would have taken both holes.

"Even with the flak I said yes to the side bet and we teed off. To make a long story they sent me tight through the pipes. I never saw two golfers make such a shift. Big Sal got longer and tighter and Sam, the little bastard, started laying five irons a foot, two feet, three feet from every pin. Goodbye eight hundred and a little more."

"I learned one thing that day, something I thought I already knew—keep your eyes open. These guys were *good*. They fooled the hell out of me. They hustled the hustler.

"I saw them a couple times since, and one time I asked for a rematch. Same setup but I wanted strokes. They didn't hear me."

Petrie makes a comfortable living each year, pulling in from between fifteen and twenty-five thousand, "before taxes."

Taxes?

"I write off expenses."

Petrie is not a big-time gambler, nor is he small time. He's somewhere in the middle, and he's happy about where he is. He says he could never stand the pressure of the super hustlers.

Former U.S.G.A. President Richard Tufts, known as Mr. Golf, was quoted recently in *Par Golf* as saying that "Americans have become a nation of nudgers. We want everything to be as easy as possible for us and no longer have the fortitude to play the ball of life as it lies."

He was referring to the state of amateur golf and in particular to Don Petrie and his friends, the hustler and the manager. "The hustler," says Tufts, "quite often is scrupulous about his handicap. In fact, it isn't necessary for him to play with an inflated handicap because he is a solid, experienced player who knows exactly what he can do."

He went on to say that the hustler, unlike most amateur golfers, will play his ball out of high rough, divots and will not take eighteen-inch gimmee putts. He would rather play the game as it should be played.

The manager, on the other hand, says Tufts, "is dishonest. By rigging his handicap to take advantage of another golfer, he reveals a basic lack of integrity. Winning is everything and he stacks the deck in his favor. He takes his opponent for a dummy. It may take a little time to get onto the mamager, but inevitably his real game is discovered and he runs out of pigeons."

There were many pigeons taken in the most infamous of all betting scandals at Deepdale Country Club on Long Island in 1955, in which two New Jersey players got involved in a $45,000 Calcutta.

Calcuttas are team matches which are auctioned off to club members. The two Jersey men arrived at Deepdale and told the members they played to an 18 and 17 handicap respectively, and then proceeded to bet on themselves. They won easily since their real handicap was three. Someone in the crowd recognized them, but relayed the information too late. The men had already collected their winnings and gone home.

As a result of the fiasco, the U.S.G.A. outlawed Calcuttas forever, though at some clubs they are still held secretly.

On the individual level everyone knows about Bobby "the second worst thing in the world is betting on a golf game and losing, the worst is not betting at all" Riggs. But golf is his second sport.

The real links dinosaurs are men like Martin Stanovich, The Fat Man, who looked like a Weight Watchers reject who stumbled on the course by mistake, but in actuality would, as Lee Trevino put it, "Sixty-eight you to death—a hell of a player."

Then there was Stanley Tannenbaum who the night before a match would memorize hysterical one-liners and deliver them to his opponent the next day. With fantastic results. How about Charley the Blade who played with only a four iron, the Stork who played with one leg tied behind him, and the Whiskey Drinker who drank from a flask and played drunk for the first nine, and then at ten, when his opponent jumped at doubling the stakes, would miraculously sober up and take the guy to the cleaners.

It's been said—and who's to refute it—that the money bet on golf courses in any given year not only tops the combined total of all money bet on all other sports but would also pay for the defense budget. It follows, therefore, that in golf, which no one bets on the professional level, just about everybody bets on the amateur level.

As a rich man's game, golf also has its share of upper-crust gamblers who bet for the sport of it. They prefer betting on the professionals, but with a twist.

Ben was born and bred in a small, beachside Connecticut town, in a 25-room bungalow, by a nanny, a live-in maid, and his parents whom he saw very little of. As payment for their absence during his childhood they had been making it up to him by doling out rather large sums of money each month.

Ben proudly announced in the clubhouse at the PGA in Cleveland that he was a "free-lance liver" whose only job was to keep it that way. He had just turned thirty-four. His partner, an investment banker named Randy, grew up in Alabama, went to voice-training school in Atlanta to get rid of his drawl, and when he worked did so in Chicago. He told me his whole life was a study in upward mobility.

Randy had flown in three days before the tournament, his eighth of the year. Once a month Randy would call Ben or vice versa, and they'd decide which tournament they'd go to. The Glen Campbell was their first of the year, followed by the United Airlines-Ontario Open, The Jackie Gleason, the Doral, the Tournament of Champions, the Colonial, and the Western Open. The others they watched on television from their living rooms and on the phone to each other. Five minutes before each telecast one would make a long distance call to the other and remain on the line till the last shot was made.

"A fifty-dollar phone call is insignificant by comparison," Ben said simply.

What Ben and Randy did in front of the tube and on the course was bet. On anything. On who would win before the round began, who would win the tournament itself, what scores by individual players would be, whether Trevino would beat Player, whether Jim Jewell would beat John Jacobs. Once Randy had money on Bunky Henry plus two strokes to beat Jim Wiechers. It wasn't until the next day that he found out Bunky had missed the cut and hadn't played at all.

"I suppose I should have read the papers, but really, we've got so many bets going it's impossible to keep track."

The "generalities," as Randy called them—the bets on who would win, etc.—were taken care of before the round. The "specialities" were much more fun. One of Ben's favorites was which side of the pin the ball would land on.

"He's awfully good at that," Randy conceded, "and unless I feel particularly lucky I won't take it." Randy's big gun is another in the either-or category: will the putt sink or no? "Casper, for example, is an extraordinary putter, so naturally the odds will go down. Of course everything depends upon the variables: how long is the putt, how has he been putting thus far, is it a particularly difficult putt? Ben and I talk it over and arrive at the fairest estimation."

Neither one plays much golf, although at one time they shot regularly in the high eighties. "You might say we've made golf truly a spectator sport. First, the game is one of the slowest in existence, which makes it possible to isolate just about everything, down to the last shot. Second, its not necessary to focus on one player. I've gotten bored watching Nicklaus. What we do is shoot over to the next hole. Third, and this is most important, I am constantly thinking. There are no lulls in the action. There may be in the game itself, but never in me. There's too much going on."

In 1972, when they attended fourteen tournaments, their total handle, Randy estimated, was over $400,000.

Ben leaned over the table. "That probably sounds like a lot, right? It's not. When we totaled it all up Randy was ahead, what, twelve thousand?"

"Just about."

In 1973, their third year on the tour, through the PGA, Ben was doing well, up by more than $40,000. Randy said he had a dream a few nights before in which he saw Ben behind bars in debtors' prison. "Which obviously means the tide is changing."

On the third day, Saturday, August 11, the three of us walked out on the course looking for Johnny Miller.

The day before Miller had shot a one over 72, with three bogies on the back and a birdie on number seven. They checked the charts Randy carried with him in a briefcase. Inside the case were dividers, A through Z. They learned that Miller was sixth on the money list, that he was generally a slow starter and good in the stretch (they based that on Miller's closing-day 63 to win the U.S. Open) and that the young pro was steady.

"For us there are two avenues of excitement: one, that the golfer is naturally a fine player who will provide a good day's entertainment, like Miller; on the other hand, someone who is erratic is just as exciting from a betting standpoint. The possibility of a rookie getting an 80 makes the betting just as erratic."

On the second hole, Miller had to make a thirty-five-foot putt for a bird. Ben bet he would, Randy gave him 10 to 1 for $50. The putt started high and broke suddenly down toward the hole. For a second it looked as if it would slide by, but at the last moment it turned and dropped.

Ben threw his arms in the air, let out a whoop and marked $500 in his notepad. Randy also made a notation in his. It wasn't that they didn't trust one another. Double-checking was always the best policy.

Miller parred the next five holes, very boring for Ben and Randy, so they walked over to the tenth to watch Palmer. Arnie had blown to a 76 the day before and had already ruined whatever chances he had of a comeback by taking a 38 on the front side.

Ben discovered from someone who had been following Palmer that Arnie had taken nineteen putts on the front side.

"Well," said Ben, "no doubt we can't bet on whether he'll make them. He won't."

"Simple, then." Randy was already counting his money. "We'll bet on which side the putt will slide by on."

"Agreed."

I wondered if there were others like them.

"Of course," Ben said matter of factly. "Tarcher."

"Tarcher." Randy spoke the name as if it were an old debt he never paid. "He's sick."

Ben went on. "Tarcher and his friends spend half their lives on the tour, more than some of the players. They're all wealthy and have been doing it for years. You have to remember though that all the money they bet never goes beyond the confines of their little group. I would estimate there's about twelve of them and they bet, what, over two million a year."

"Easily."

"They tried to incorporate us in 1972. Never! They bet for blood, we have fun."

Randy said there were at least fifty men and women involved in the "generality" and "specialty" gambling on the tour. "And that's extremely conservative."

I left them in the clubhouse after the round. Ben was the

winner, pocketing $800. He bought the drinks and dinner and offered me some advice. "Bet for the love of it and never to catch up. Then it becomes a sickness. There's something inherently negative about catch-up gambling. You send out bad vibrations which cut your chances for winning in half."

I left them at the table, each with a notebook in his hands, writing in the day's tabulations and making a side bet on what the check would come to.

5
The Women

"You want to know what their trouble is? They're too goddamn slow!"

Burgess Lange, who spoke this wisdom, is a Washington, D.C., government official and member of the Burning Tree Club in nearby Bethesda, Md. He doesn't have to worry about it though, since Burning Tree is one of those male-only country clubs sprinkled about the country. In fact, the only time women are allowed on the grounds is just before Christmas, when they are allowed into the pro shops to buy gifts for their husbands.

Lange's attitude is similar to what a professor of Elizabethan literature once told me: "First there was man, then there was woman, or wo-man, or woe to man." If statistics don't lie and if men's concepts of women in sports are what they seem to be, that little ditty is still very much alive today.

But things are changing.

A few years ago the idea of a girl Little Leaguer or a woman jockey was too absurd to even consider. The sports were too tough for fragile ladies to play, and especially if they had to play against men.

In the last couple of years though, with fem-lib, sexual liberation, and Billie Jean King, women have begun strapping on their sportsgear and giving men a run for their money and their masculine egos.

In golf, women have not been as subjected to ridicule as they have in other sports, primarily because golf is not as physically demanding, and also because, for as long as anyone can remember, women have been relegated to their own separate existence on the links.

If women are allowed on the course to begin with, they have separate facilities, play only with each other, are often allowed to play only on certain days and at certain times, and are forbidden to enter the club's stag bar, the only place, except for the dining room, where one can buy a drink.

These problems affect women on the professional tour as well. The women who work or live on the tour fall into three categories: the pros themselves, the wives of the men pros, and a third group which has been called a lot of things—camp followers, groupies, birdies. They travel the tour like elegant gypsies searching for love or money, or both.

Bud Erickson, Executive Director of the Ladies Professional Golf Association, sits in his Atlanta office with his two Charlottes, Ivey his executive secretary and Goulding his regular one.

"The ladies' tour is an exacting life," he said, "and an interesting one, and there's a lot more interest now than ever before."

The total prize money for the 1971 tour was $520,000, and in 1973 it jumped to almost $2,000,000. The reason, says Erickson, is that sponsors are finally seeing the light: more women are taking to the fairways than ever before. The number of women playing 15 rounds or more during 1972 was 85,000 more than the previous year, bringing the total of active women golfers to 2,228,000, which represents 21.4 percent of all active golfers in the country, according to National Golf Foundation.

The more women golfers, figured big manufacturers, the more they'd be willing to turn on their televisions to watch big tournaments. And, incidentally, to buy the products advertised between the shots.

The first big manufacturer to stage a major money tournament was Sealy in 1971. The purse was $50,000.

Colgate-Palmolive followed suit in 1973 with the Dinah Shore Winners Circle Championship, the ante up to $135,000. The total cost, including promotion, ran over $3,000,000, which Colgate-Palmolive president David Foster wrote off as "an expense we would put behind our products in any event."

It was a profitable maneuver for both the manufacturers and women professionals. All of a sudden many top pros no longer had to rely on their tour winnings to survive. Their faces began popping up on TV commercials and product endorsements in magazines. It was about time.

Male pros had been adorning the media for years, pushing everything from golf balls to Cadillacs. On top of that they'd been socking away tour earnings so disproportionate to what the women made that it seemed as if there was a major and minor league of golf, based on sex alone.

For example, in 1972 on the LPGA tour, Kathy Whitworth was the leading money winner with $65,063 in 29 tournaments. The same year Jack Nicklaus led the men pros with $320,542 in 19 tournaments. A greater discrepancy occurs further down the money list. The 50th leading money earner on the women's tour was Carole Jo Skala, who won $3792, while on the men's it was Bob Lunn with $51,114.

Admittedly, the men's tour gets more attention, a fact which manufacturers feel will push more of their products.

But one point came across very clearly in 1973—everybody, both the men and women, made a lot more money. The differences between 1973 and the previous year on the women's tour in particular are testimony to that fact.

Bud Erickson said that 1973 was by far the best year ever.

* Television coverage doubled from under ten days in 1972 to over 20 in 1973, thanks to manufacturing entrepreneurs and the emergence of women from their status as second-class citizens.

* The number of tournaments rose from 21 to 36, four of which were in the $100,000-plus category, as opposed to one the year before. Included were the thirteen-week LPGA Classic on Hughes Sports Network (Jan. 8–April 29) and tournament coverage for the Sears Classic (March 24–25), the Colgate-Dinah Shore event (April 14–15), the Sealy-Fabergé Classic (June 1–2), and the USGA Women's Open (July 23).

Oscar Fraley, who writes a column for *Golf Digest,* had this to say about the USGA Women's Open and why women could never hope to compete with men: "If the women pros want me to tell them where they can go, I do have a suggestion. They should storm the bastions of the U.S. Golf Association and demand admission to the U.S. Open Championship (the men's event). 'Open' should mean open to all comers who have the qualifying talent: man, woman, child, Sam Snead, or Marilynn Smith, even though it is to be doubted that any woman would make the cut."

Thank you, Oscar.

* Another new development in 1973 was the establishment of a qualifying school for potential tour players. The first school was held in January during the Burdine's tournament and eight players qualified to come on tour and compete for their player's cards in the regular fashion. A second school was held during the summer.

Just because the LPGA has made major strides in the last couple of years revamping the pro tour, the women themselves are viewed by male sportswriters as they've always been—pieces of cheesecake. How about this for the title of a lead article on Marlene Hagge by *Golf Digest*'s senior editor John May: How ABOUT ROUNDS OF 35-23-36? MARLENE HAS THEM.

The three pictures accompanying the article are in keeping with the title: in one she is holding an all-day sucker, in another she's leaning, like the White Rock Ginger Ale girl, over a pond in a white bikini, and the third is a typical face shot, hair flowing about.

Marlene Hagge is one of the old-school pros. She's been on the tour for twenty-four years, having started in 1950 at sixteen years old. She was the youngest woman ever to win an LPGA event at eighteen. Her career winnings total more than $250,000.

Like many touring pros, both male and female, she chose at an early age between a heavy social life and golf. Since her father was a pro himself, she concentrated on golf and began piling up victories. At eleven, for instance, she won the Long Beach, California, junior championship against boys up to the age of fifteen.

When she hit the tour there were only seven regulars—Peggy Kirk Bell, Patty Berg, the late Babe Zaharias, Betty Jameson, Louise Suggs, and Marilynn Smith—the only one still playing with any regularity.

Marlene Hagge, as part of the old guard at forty, is up against the challenges of teenagers who threaten to dethrone her.

The most popular and exciting of the young stars is a nineteen-year-old giant killer named Laura Baugh. In her first pro tournament she copped second-prize money of $2480, not exactly what Gentle Ben Crenshaw got on his initial start, but enough to earmark her as the hottest new face on the women's tour.

The press has been playing up her face and her body, but as Kathy Whitworth remarked, "The glamour thing is fine; it's got to help the tour. The nice thing about Laura, though, is that she can *play!*"

Laura, like Marlene and most of the other regular tour members, came from a home with an athletic father. Hale Baugh II, is a Cocoa Beach, Florida, attorney, West Point graduate, a U.S. Olympic team pentathlon champ in 1948, and the number one member on the University of Florida golf team that included Tommy Aaron and Dave Ragan. Unlike Hagge's father, who told her to play golf, Baugh's father merely showed her how to do it. The rest was up to her.

When her parents divorced in 1967, she went to California with her mother, where at fifteen she won the Los Angeles women's title. A year later, in 1971, she became the youngest person ever to win the U.S. Amateur championship. It was a big year for another reason—she was elected Homecoming Queen at her Long Beach high school.

One of the reasons why only 15 percent of the regular tour pros are married is reflected in an interview with Laura Baugh in *Golf Magazine*. She said she seldom dates on the tour because she feels she must be in bed by ten in order to play well the next day. "Sunday nights, when we can finally relax, everything's usually closed down, so we can't go out anyway."

On the men's tour the pros take their wives with them. On the women's tour that does not happen. The women are virtually shut off from male companionship other than tournament officials and club members. Hardly the way to form a meaningful relationship.

The women travel about 50,000 miles a year if they play with any frequency, and the pressures have been getting to some of them. Mickey Wright, the 1973 Dinah Shore winner, doesn't plan to enter many tournaments, even though the win was her first since 1969. "I skipped 22 tournaments last year," she said, "and I might skip as many this year. About the only thing I really want to do in golf is win a fifth U.S. Open."

Having Mickey Wright absent from most tournaments is like having Nicklaus or Trevino not showing up. The tournament sponsors have one less superstar to hype the public on.

A different kind of star rose in 1973, the kind the LPGA would rather forget about. Her name, Jane Blalock; her offence, allegedly advancing her ball marker on a green; the penalty imposed by the LPGA, a one-year suspension from the tour.

Ms. Blalock countered with a $2,000,000 lawsuit against the LPGA, and Atlanta judge Charles A Moye, Jr. threw out the suspension, saying it was a violation of antitrust laws for fellow golfers to make such a judgment. And later, when the LPGA appealed to a New Orleans judge to overturn the Atlanta decision, they met with no luck.

Many people think the LPGA Executive committee should

not have tried exercising their authority to such a great degree. The LPGA, on the other hand, wants supreme control over the golfers' actions. Otherwise, their thinking goes, where would the LPGA be? In the Blalock case, it's nowhere.

An unfortunate side effect occured when tour veteran Sandra Palmer, a close friend of Ms. Blalock, commented, "There are two sides to everything." The Executive Committee took it as an affront to their authority and placed *her* on a one-year suspension for "statements detrimental to the LPGA and against the code of ethics." If the LPGA couldn't get Blalock, they sure as hell would get Palmer.

Characteristic of what the board feels about rebels in the ranks, Tournament Committeemember Pam Barnett made this side-door comment when praising Laura Baugh: "Laura's great for the tour . . . the press is really going after her, but the more coverage she gets, the better it is for us: it gets the subject off our lawsuit. We've gotten a lot of publicity out of that thing, but I don't think it's been good publicity.

"Laura seems more dedicated then most of the rookies we get. Of course, that age group right under me is so rebellious. They—the group I'm talking about is, oh, eighteen to twenty-six—they don't seem to care what happens to the organization."

Pam Barnett is not far from being right. After all, the LPGA, like the PGA for men, doesn't do very much for the pros except schedule the tournaments and sign contracts with clubs, sponsors, and television. What the LPGA doesn't seem to realize is that they don't own the golfers; they don't support them monetarily, as professional team franchisers do, but the LPGA still wants the control over the women that the pro teams have.

That Jane Blalock moved her marker may be true, and if so, she should be fined for it. But to levy a year's suspension was ridiculous, and in doing so, the LPGA, via Blalock's countersuit, has lost rather than gained.

The women professionals are independent: most of them rely on their winnings and product endorsements to stay alive: the few with husbands dip into his kitty every so often in order to remain on the tour. Others use family money. But for the most part women golf professionals are a breed of people who rely on their own talents to make it, and not on males to keep them going.

Money winnings by women pros as compared to the men counterparts should cause us to listen a little more closely to Bella Abzug and less to certain male congressionals who would rather keep the status quo. Although the great percentage of males will look with envy upon someone like Kathy Whitworth, who is fast approaching the half million mark. In fifteen years as a pro she has gathered in exactly $488,318, which averages out to around $36,000 a year, and that's only in "official" money. Add to that two or three hundred thousand more from unofficial events and endorsements and you've got a fairly wealthy woman. In 1973 alone she won $85,209. Unfortunately that would be good for only 30th place on the men's tour.

In 1948, when Ben Hogan had a pretty good year with $32,112, the great Babe Zaharias won top money at—you guessed it—$3400.

Past Money Leaders

Year	Player	Money
1948	Babe Zaharias	$ 3,400
1949	Babe Zaharias	4,650
1950	Babe Zaharias	14,800
1951	Babe Zaharias	15,087
1952	Betsy Rawls	14,505
1953	Louise Suggs	19,816
1954	Patty Berg	16,011
1955	Patty Berg	16,497
1956	Marlene Hagge	20,235

Year	Player	Money
1957	Patty Berg	16,272
1958	Beverly Hanson	12,639
1959	Betsy Rawls	26,774
1960	Louise Suggs	16,892
1961	Mickey Wright	22,236
1962	Mickey Wright	21,641
1963	Mickey Wright	31,269

1964

Player	Money
1. Mickey Wright	$29,800
2. Ruth Jessen	23,431
3. Kathy Whitworth	20,434
4. Betsy Rawls	19,350
5. Marlene Hagge	18,843
6. Shirley Englehorn	18,582
7. Sandra Haynie	17,061
8. Clifford Ann Creed	15,443
9. Mary Mills	13,963
10. Marilynn Smith	12,738

1965

Player	Money
1. Kathy Whitworth	$28,658
2. Marlene Hagge	21,532
3. Carol Mann	20,875
4. Clifford Ann Creed	20,795

Player	Money
5. Sandra Haynie	17,722
6. Marilynn Smith	16,692
7. Mary Mills	13,007
8. Susie Maxwell	12,982
9. Judy Torluemke	12,237
10. Betsy Rawls	10,898

1966

Player	Money
1. Kathy Whitworth	$33,517
2. Sandra Haynie	30,157
3. Mickey Wright	26,672
4. Carol Mann	23,246
5. Clifford Ann Creed	21,089
6. Marilynn Smith	16,412
7. Judy Torluemke	15,180
8. Judy Kimball	13,571
9. Shirley Englehorn	13,405
10. Mary Mills	12,823

1967

Player	Money
1. Kathy Whitworth	$32,937
2. Sandra Haynie	26,543
3. Carol Mann	24,666
4. Mickey Wright	20,613
5. Susie Maxwell	19,537

Player	*Money*
6. Clifford Ann Creed	17,940
7. Judy Kimball	14,722
8. Marilynn Smith	13,045
9. Shirley Englehorn	11,786
10. Margee Masters	11,725

1968

Player	*Money*
1. Kathy Whitworth	$48,379
2. Carol Mann	45,921
3. Sandra Haynie	25,992
4. Marilynn Smith	20,945
5. Sandra Spuzich	19,325
6. Clifford Ann Gordon	17,619
7. Mickey Wright	17,147
8. Sandra Palmer	16,906
9. Shirley Englehorn	15,579
10. Donna Caponi	14,563

1969

Player	*Money*
1. Carol Mann	$49,152
2. Kathy Whitworth	48,171
3. Donna Caponi	30,067
4. Shirley Englehorn	24,486
5. Sandra Haynie	24,276
6. Sandra Spuzich	20,339

Player	Money
7. Susie Berning	19,966
8. Murle Lindstrom	19,630
9. Sandra Palmer	18,319
10. Mickey Wright	17,851

1970

Player	Money
1. Kathy Whitworth	$30,235
2. Sandra Haynie	26,626
3. Shirley Englehorn	22,727
4. Marilynn Smith	22,391
5. Judy Rankin	22,195
6. Carol Mann	20,907
7. Donna Caponi	19,369
8. Sandra Palmer	18,424
9. Betsy Rawls	17,897
10. Mary Mills	15,055

1971

Player	Money
1. Kathy Whitworth	$41,181
2. Sandra Haynie	36,219
3. Jane Blalock	34,492
4. Sandra Palmer	34,035
5. Donna Caponi	23,069
6. JoAnne Carner	21,604
7. Jo Ann Prentice	20,138

Player	Money
8. Pam Barnett	18,801
9. Judy Rankin	17,294
10. Marlene Hagge	16,514

1972

Player	Money
1. Kathy Whitworth	$65,063
2. Jane Blalock	57,323
3. Judy Rankin	49,183
4. Betty Burfeindt	47,548
5. Sandra Haynie	39,701
6. Kathy Ahern	38,072
7. Sandra Palmer	36,715
8. Carol Mann	36,452
9. Marilynn Smith	29,910
10. Jo Ann Prentice	27,583

1973

Player	Money
1. Kathy Whitworth	$85,209
2. Judy Rankin	74,913
3. Sandra Palmer	60,186
4. Betty Burfeindt	53,312
5. Carol Mann	48,325
6. Mary Mills	49,977
7. Sandra Haynie	48,929

Player	Money
8. Kathy Cornelius	45,801
9. Jane Blalock	43,915
10. Joyce Kazmierski	42,241

All-Time Money Leaders

Player	Money
1. Kathy Whitworth	$488,318
2. Mickey Wright	327,863
3. Sandra Haynie	312,829
4. Carol Mann	300,853
5. Betsy Rawls	293,406
6. Marlene Hagge	273,543
7. Marilynn Smith	268,319
8. Judy Rankin	231,108
9. Sandra Palmer	200,044
10. Jo Ann Prentice	196,741
11. Louise Suggs	187,814
12. Patty Berg	187,812
13. Mary Mills	183,997
14. Clifford Ann Creed	170,201
15. Kathy Cornelius	157,168

A One Iron from the Laundry Room

Wives of male golf pros fall on the other end of the spectrum. Unlike the women pros, a wife relies totally on her husband's earnings while at the same time catering to his need for a wife, homemaker, mother to his children, companion, and general clean-up.

Chauvinism lives in the classic sense of the word, but it is neither exclusively the man's nor woman's fault. They both share equal billing.

As I watched the wives sitting around white lawn tables and in the clubhouse, doing needlepoint and talking about nothing in particular, I was reminded of all the great wars in history in which the women huddled together waiting for their men to come home from battle.

It makes little difference on the tour whether she's the wife of a star like Nicklaus or one of the rookies. The attitude is just about the same; they've all gone through their husbands' ups and downs. Some have made it big, others are still trying to.

Linda Knight, whose husband, Dwaine, was a rookie on the '73 tour, talked with me in the press tent at the Sammy Davis, Jr. Open in Hartford. Dwaine had just qualified. She was in a positive mood.

Linda had married Dwaine three months before and began traveling with him. "To marry a rookie or rabbit," she said, "you've got to have a lot going, because there's no security in it at all. If the girl is insecure herself and has to have at least $30,000 a year, a home, everything lined out for her with no risk involved, she'd never make it out here.

"You've got to believe, you've got to believe in your husband, you have to be optimistic, you have to roll with the punches, and you can't worry about where your next meal is coming from because if you do, then that's an added pressure on him. It's miserable that way, and it ends up the two of you will fight and the marriage will, you know . . . "

It's that kind of devotion, according to many reliable sources, that puts money in the golfers' pockets. When the pro has a stable home life, his game will automatically inherit a lot of the stability it takes to win.

Frank Beard, a married man, came up with these statistics: "There were twenty-six different golfers who won championships on the tour last year, and of those twenty-six, only one was single—Miller Barber. Of the top twenty money winners last year, Mr. X was the only bachelor. Of the guys who've done well so far this year, the only bachelors are Miller and Raymond Floyd. I don't know the exact number of bachelors playing the tour, but I'll bet anything that the percentage of bachelors among the golfers who miss the cut each week is a helluva lot higher than the percentage of bachelors among the golfers who finish in the top ten."

Beard was talking about 1970. The top thirty money winners of 1972 were all married.

Nobody on the tour can think of someone's game going to hell after he got married, but there are those whose games came together as a result of it. Jerry Heard and Champagne Tony Lema were playing terrible golf until they got married. Heard in particular felt a lot of pressure when he realized he'd have to feed one more mouth, but he said it helped him, gave him more responsibility.

On the other hand, Bruce Crampton almost went off the deep end when he and his wife began seriously considering divorce.

In early 1973 Crampton picked up back-to-back victories at Phoenix and Tucson, for a total of $60,000. Ironically, it was during the two tournaments that Crampton and his wife Joan were having all the trouble. The pressure mounted during the next three weeks and finally came to a head at the Andy Williams in San Diego.

On the final day of the tournament Crampton was leading after 15 holes when, to the astonishment of the crowd, he suddenly collapsed. He bogied fifteen, sixteen and seventeen, and missed a short putt on eighteen. He finished third.

Jim Kelly, a broadcaster with NBC monitor and close friend of Crampton, was there. "The fans were completely aghast at the total collapse of this man who had won two tournaments. They couldn't understand it, but of course they didn't know his personal problems at the time.

"I think it's important to realize that these fellas, even though they're independent businessmen, are human beings just like everybody else. They have upset stomachs just like we do, they get hung-over just like we do and they have problems with their wives or their girl friends."

The emotional strain felt by the pros is also felt by their wives. A lot of them refuse to follow their husbands around on the course because they get so caught up in his game that they're a wreck by the time eighteen comes around.

Linda Knight would rather be with her husband. "The wife should be out there, you know, she's got to be able to want to follow him around. When he bogies she's got to have a smile on her face when he looks over and his face is down to his knees. She's got to be there on the eighteenth green to say, 'That's all right, honey, you shot a good round.'

"It's almost as if my whole life's absorbed into his."

Linda, like many of the wives, comes from a comfortable background and had to make major adjustments when she hit the tour. "My father is a doctor and we lived pretty well. Out here on the tour it's a whole different story.

"The thing I find most difficult to be pleasant about is loading the car. We've got this refrigerator we carry with us, and everything else but the kitchen sink. Loading the car at three or four in the morning and then driving twelve hours, and then unloading it is tough. But I can adjust. I *had* to adjust. I never realized before how disheartening it is out here.

"When Dwaine was back home he was always happy and gay. I never thought of him getting down. I'm an extreme optimist, so I've had to adjust to the fact that he has to be pushed sometimes."

With all their leisure time, coupled with the fact that their husbands play a game they themselves could play, surprisingly few wives swing their own clubs.

The reason, say the women, is a fear of competition. Just as they won't tell their husbands what club they should have used when their shots have gone short or long, they also won't be in the same field. "I know if I was in the same field as my husband," says Linda, "I would tell him how to play his game. No man would stand for anybody telling him how to do his job, especially his wife. I would resent it if I had finished nursing and he came in and told me how to give an injection or bathe the patient.

"What he does feed off though is my energy and my optimism. I'm good for him that way."

Where do the pros find these apple-pie and motherhood women? A lot of them marry childhood sweethearts, some airline stewardesses, and others meet them on the course or in the clubhouse where the women work as volunteers.

Seldom are the wives worldly. They've come from—if not sheltered—at least secular backgrounds. They've not been exposed to the hype and hyperbole of big-city living. They prefer reading *True Romance* to *Time*, are education rather than anthropology majors in college, and their moral fiber has a Middle American toughness to it.

They often see their existence as a sacrificial one. Tradition motivates them, and they are determined to fill "the woman's place" in society.

A Piece of the Action

A third group of women, smaller than the other two, is more diversified. It is characterized, among other things, by independent wealth, the need to travel, and a desire to mingle with well-known sports figures.

Enter the golf groupie.

One would think that groupies—or birdies—would go after the out-and-out swingers on the tour like Ray Floyd and Doug Sanders. Not altogether true, as I was to find out at the '73 PGA in Cleveland.

It was a beautiful starting day. Everything was stark —the greens were emerald colored, the golfers, in their pastel outfits and three-month tans, looked magnificent. The entire operation was running according to plan.

I'd left the Somerset Inn a half hour before, stopped by the press tent for a cup of coffee and then taken a short stroll around the clubhouse toward the first tee.

I stood on the practice green waiting for Jack Nicklaus to come out for his starting time. When you stand on the practice green you either watch the players drop putts, which gets boring after twenty or thirty, or watch girls, which never gets boring.

They were more beautiful than in Westchester the week before, more blonde and more hometown. I once wrote a hundred-page book proposal and sent it to my agent. He called me the next day with an interesting piece of information. Every single one of the girls in the proposal was a blonde. "Even the villainess," he told me. My head must be back in antiquity somewhere, when blonde meant pure, and not-blonde meant not so pure.

I talked with a pro who asked not to be identified because of his wife. He was speculating on one of his favorite tour subjects—the golf groupie. In other sports, he said, especially football, where camp followers truck along after their pros, there is a built-in star system. To have slept with a top ballplayer is a major accomplishment for the groupies—they have something to tell their friends.

"I know some of them out here—different class of women. At a golf tournament, like the club members and officials, they are much more sophisticated. They have college educations, and don't come on like some big fuck like the football groupies.

"There's not much prostitution here, but I know of one case where a girl—I think it was the Western Open—offered her body for fifty a throw. About a half-dozen guys took her up on it."

I asked him to point out a groupie to me. He said he'd rather not. But as we walked to the first tee he stopped, looked hard in the direction of the fourth green (which rolled back in toward the first tee), and said, "There's one of them, the blonde." Another one. "She likes only the top ten money winners, or that's what she says. I mean it, she won't even look if the guy is lower then tenth."

How do you approach a girl who likes only the top golfers, when all you're doing is writing a book on them? I ambled over to the fourth green where Lanny Wadkins, the Golden Bearcub, was putting out.

Wadkins was third in money for the year. A prime target.

There was my blonde, elegant, long hair falling over nut-brown shoulders. She wasn't the twenty-year-old she looked from a distance—more like thirty, thin, with a taut face, skin stretching back toward her ears. The short yellow skirt and matching top gave her an aura of class. Just right for Canterbury—not at all out of place, but still standing out.

And her eyes—riveted on Wadkins, short, stocky, lining up his putt on the par-three hole. Wadkins knew she was watching, maybe not her in particular, but certainly a lot of other nubile young things. Aside from his powerful, compact swing and steady, head-down march up the fairways, Lanny has another habit which differentiates him from most other pros. Every so often he brings his right hand to his curly blond hair and twitches the curl that falls over his forehead. What is it? Knowing he's in the spotlight? In front of 5,000,000 viewers? Looking for more product endorsements?

The girl, following him from the green toward the fifth tee, hitched up her skirt and remained just a few feet behind.

Seldom have I seen such determination in a woman's face —except at a prizefight. In that sweaty, noisy mad arena where two half-naked gladiators battle to the death, women's faces glisten with passion. Masturbating, rubbing their bodies openly, these women send heated vibrations toward the ring where their surrogate lovers battle one another. The sweat pours from their faces like undulating waterfalls from below their neatly coiffed hairdos.

It's not quite the same on the course, though, not with my blonde. She's cool, never bothering to edge up to her target. She will follow him around and hope that somewhere during the 6800 yards he will spot her and walk close beside her.

"Excuse me," I asked her on the 500-yard sixth. "I'm doing a book on the tour and I'd like to ask you some questions on the gallery reaction."

For a moment, just for a moment, she hesitated. Was I trying to pick her up? Then she spotted my tape recorder and press badge. I must be for real. "Of course, but do you mind if we walk along?"

Nothing at all like that hooker who takes on football teams in Detroit, or the pretty young seventeen-year-old part-time porno queen who loves the New York Mets and tried once to be their first batgirl. Not Gerry, my blonde.

"First I'd like to ask you about yourself, where you came from, what your husband does. You know, the kind of people who frequent tournaments."

With the tape recorder resting in my right hand I moved the mike closer to her thin, delicate lips.

"Tucson, Arizona."

"And your husband, what does he do? What do you do?"

"I'm no longer married. Divorced. I don't do very much in the way of working. Designing jewelry, costume jewelry."

"Do you play golf?"

"Not like him," she smiled, nodding towards Lanny. Small lines formed around her eyes.

"Is this your first tournament?" I asked. I had to ask again.

"Oh no, I've been to, let's see, Doral, Inverrary, Pebble Beach, all the California tournaments, and last week at Westchester, here, and, well, I'll skip the USI next week, but I'll be at the Liggett and Myers in North Carolina and the Hartford, and then we'll see."

Who needs a tournament schedule? Just ask Gerry.

She's no dummy; she knew the game, at least on the cerebral level. Knew what club Wadkins was going to hit. During the conversation she reeled off statistics with the aplomb of a book-maker talking with an old-time sportswriter. Right down to height and weight of some of the players, their tour records, what place they finished. Their favorite food.

Like the mysterious old lady in Camus' *The Stranger*, who shows up at all the courtroom trials for no apparent reason other than that she had nothing else to do, Gerry's habit was golf. How did she pick golf as her sport?

"Fresh air, walking around with the golfers. What other sport is there where the audience can travel along with the player? None I can think of."

"Do you know any of the golfers personally?"

"How do you mean?" A little suspicious.

"By this time, with all the tournaments you've been to, you must have bumped into them."

She smiled again. "It's awfully funny—that's not really the word—attractive would be more like it. The golfers are not at all like other sports personalities. The others are rough and tumble, perspiring, banging into one another. Golfers are gentle, if you know what I mean. Awfully conservative, too. Even shy, some of them.

"If I walked up to a football player and said hello, he'd ask me for my name, phone number, and where I'll be after the game, all in ten seconds. The golfers don't do that. They shy away, or at most ask me how I'm enjoying myself. They really care about the people watching them. Not that other sports personalities don't care, but, you see, when they're on the field, they have no contact with the audience. They hear them, and that's about all.

"On the tour there's a little joking around, and when one of them makes a fine shot, the gallery can walk up and congratulate them. It's much more personal, don't you think?"

I do. But what to say next. I wanted to get in deeper, but couldn't afford to blow it. "Are there a lot of gallery members you've met who don't play that much, but like to sort of follow the tour for the reasons you've given?"

"I don't know what you mean."

I do, but how do I say it?

"Let me put it this way: when you've been traveling the tour have you run into some of the same people, men and women, who're doing the same thing, walked the same eighteen you have?"

"Oh, I don't know." She looked toward the green where Wadkins was lining up a twenty footer.

I was no longer there for her, neither was anyone else. Just

Wadkins and the ball that *had* to go in. He walked to the other side of the hole to line it up. Squatting down on his haunches, he checked the line and then rose. As he stood over the ball I saw Gerry's face twitch, popping like a small bubble in and out of her cheek. Nervous. She wanted it in as much as he did.

Wadkins laid his blade behind the ball and looked up at the hole twice.

The gallery, about three hundred strong, stood and sat quietly around the green. Their pastel outfits were still, even with the wind. From a far-off green came a cheer. The marshals, decked out in their own light blue and yellow uniforms, stood with their arms crossed inside the ropes dividing the gallery from the golfers.

Wadkins waited a moment, motionless. He needed the putt; he'd shot a 73 the first day and was playing catch-up golf. Just before he stroked the putt Gerry shook her head no. No, what?

The ball was on its way towards the hole, followed by six hundred eyes, dead on line. Gerry dropped her head, not willing to watch. If she could have led that little round ball in she would have. If she could have suddenly turned invisible and run to the green and guided it in. With her head down and arms stiff by her side she waited for the gallery reaction.

Missed. The ball slid by and Wadkins had a tap-in for a par.

The 201-yard seventh takes a left-to-right fade to stay out of trouble. We waited near the tee while the group ahead putted out.

"About the gallery members who follow the tour regularly?" I asked her.

"I have some friends, people I've met along the way, and a close friend I travel with most of the time. Jean and I room together, the others I meet here and there."

The pro who spotted Gerry in the first place mentioned her friend: "A short, black-haired girl with tremendous tits. She hangs around the motel pools a lot, mostly in the mornings, before the big names go out. What she doesn't know is sex before a round is a killer. I can't even sleep with my wife in the morning, or even the night before sometimes. It makes me tired. It's just like any athlete, I guess."

Gerry was ready to talk during the lull in the action. "It must also be the atmosphere. I'm sure of it. A country club is much nicer than a stadium, no traffic rush. And I buy a grounds' pass which allows me to eat in the clubhouse, in the dining room. When I finish eighteen I'm tired and go into the club for a drink. It's so beautiful out here. Look at it!" She was warming up. She'd never been interviewed on a course before, and she liked the questions I asked.

But I could tell she wanted to keep an eye on Wadkins, whose attention she hoped to get. Being seen with me meant she wasn't alone. She wanted to appear unattached.

"What about after the round?" I asked her. "Can I buy you a drink and talk some more?"

She hesitated for a moment.

"Look, if you have plans, maybe some other time, like to-morrow?"

"Let's see how I feel."

Okay. We agreed to meet on the eighteenth, where she would give me an answer.

Arnold Palmer was having another bad day, a two over 38 on the front side. Palmer would come in with a one over 36 on the back side for a 74, which, coupled with his 76 the previous day, caused him to miss the cut, the first time in 16 PGAs.

"Again today," he later said in the press tent, "I played like I did yesterday. I took 19 putts on the front nine. The whole game was on the greens. It was so ridiculous I couldn't even get mad—it was funny."

He said he wasn't going to play for a couple of weeks, maybe longer.

Lanny Wadkins came in with a 69, which put him three strokes off the pace set by Mason Rudolph. I was glad to see Mason in the lead. He hadn't been doing so well on the '73 tour, having won just over $21,000 through the Canadian Open. He was one of the first pros I sort of rubbed elbows with when I was a high-school player. My coach, John L. Sullivan, was a good friend of his, and used to talk about him quite often.

Mason is one of those pros who seldom wins but has stuck it out on the tour for fifteen years. His career winnings have not yet reached the half-million mark, which means he's averaged under $30,000 a year. In 1972 it was $27,345.

For a guy who's been around so long his name doesn't conjure up very much response. The motel where he stayed for the PGA wouldn't let him register until he sent a week's advance check, and when the press corps heard that he was the current leader they voted not to have a formal mass interview in the press tent. It didn't matter that he put together his two-under round in the worst of conditions—a twenty-five-mile-an-hour wind that the early starters missed, nor did it matter that he got out of a sick bed to do it. Mason Rudolph simply did not have enough flash to make news.

Wadkins signed his card in the small tent to the rear of the eighteenth green, autographed a few programs and hats some kids shoved in his face, and went off to the practice tee.

Gerry, looking rather pleased that her man had done well with his 69, walked over to me. "Let's have that drink."

The Canterbury clubhouse, a sprawling mass of dining rooms, banquet rooms, alcoves, and a huge patio overlooking the course was the ideal place to relax after a round. We sat at a table in the main dining room. I plugged in the tape recorder and we began.

Gerry had been following the tour for three years, attending fifteen to twenty tournaments a season. "A lot depends upon the weather, who's playing, lots of things."

"Like what?"

"Who's winning. Very important."

"You have favorites?"

"Don't you? Everyone likes winners. Last year, for instance, there was Nicklaus, who won over $300,000, but I didn't follow him that often."

"Why not?"

"Oh, many reasons. Primarily, too many others followed him.

I couldn't see anything. There was no place to go; the tees were filled, and the fairways and greens.

"Lee Trevino's always fun," she smiled, lifting the banana Daiquiri to her mouth. "He never stops talking; it's his way of relaxing. Most of the others are always silent, almost brooding to keep themselves under control. Lee jokes and carries on—he's wonderful. A lovely man."

"Do you know him personally?"

"I suppose," she said off-handedly. She obviously wanted to drop it.

At that moment I wished I had met her casually at one of the motel lounges and not told her I was doing a book. She might have opened up more. On her second drink, though, she began loosening up.

"Now, I particularly like Tom Weiskopf—he was sixth last year, of course. And the young men, Grier Jones, Jerry Heard, and certainly Lanny Wadkins."

Her friend Jean came in a while later. Jean, the one with "the big tits," was dressed almost identically to Gerry, except she was in light blue.

The conversation that followed between them was right out of a New York East Side bar between two girls comparing notes on their last 45 dates.

Gerry: "Any luck?"

Jean: "No."

Gerry: "Who were you with?"

Jean: "Dave Hill."

Gerry: "And?"

Jean: "He missed the cut."

Gerry: "Lanny had a 69."

Jean: "It was horrible. He couldn't do a thing right."

If you can't get information from the source herself about herself, someone else is just as good. The real grit about groupies —or golfies or birdies—like Jean and Gerry, I decided, could be about another girl with the same inclinations.

I took another tack. "While you've been on the tour—and I'm only speculating on this from what I've heard from the pros and caddies—are there, would you say, groupies, or golf-pro followers, on the circuit? If so, have you seen any?"

The two women looked at one another and then into my own innocent eyes.

"Well . . . " began Gerry. That was all Jean needed. She broke right in with "Ann Brody."

"Oh, God!" Gerry looked genuinely disgusted. "Have you heard of *her?*"

"No," I said, "I haven't."

"Maybe you'd better change her name."

"I will." I have.

"Locker rooms and late nights, that's her scene."

Jean was a bit younger than Gerry, softer looking, rounder. Hers was a look of supple sensuality. Gerry was cool, sophisticated.

Jean continued. "Ann—where was it, the Sahara last year. . . ?"

"Two years ago."

"Right. The locker room. Oh, do you think I should?" Jean looked at Gerry.

"Why not? I can't say I love her very much."

"Ann has a system—that's what she calls it. She would approach the caddies first, and through them to the pros. Like a lot of the girls she went after those pretty, young caddies. She figured the caddies would tell their pros about her, and then the pro would ask her out. Last year at the Sahara she got very drunk and somehow got past the guards in the locker room and took on about eight guys."

"Is that true?"

"Of course." Right from the hip.

"From what I heard she was with five, not eight," Gerry added.

"Who in particular?" I asked.

"Sorry, that won't get in your book. I like the guys. I'm talking about Ann here. Anyway"—she didn't miss a beat—"anyway, she gets in there, pulls off her clothes . . . "

"Which are awfully—what's the word?"

"Old!"

"Old."

"And she announces that she wants to take a shower, and would someone rub her back. I could hear the stampede from the tenth green."

"The guards heard the ruckus and ran in there. But nothing was done to get her out. From what I heard, she took them on too. Needless to say, the PGA people heard about it and she was barred from the tournament."

"It's like not making the cut."

"That's funny."

Jean's arms were flying about as she continued. Her black hair, half way down her back, swung freely. "She had a lot of nerve, don't you think?"

"Well, if she wanted to do it, what better way?"

"Lot better ways. The lounges in town, that's where the action is. Go to one about ten and you'll meet someone."

Gerry added, "You also find a lot of men you don't want to meet."

"Those, too, but there's usually a pro or two at the bar. They get lonely. If they're married, and their wives aren't around, well, what are they doing to do? Find someone. And then there are the bachelors."

"You mentioned lonely."

"Of course. Aren't we all? They travel around the country, week after week, like traveling salesmen. No steady girl, no real home, a different motel each week. What kind of life is that?"

Both Jean and Gerry have college educations and could get good jobs, which they won't, since they're financially independent. Jean's husband died and left her a bundle; Gerry is divorced and receives alimony and occasionally designs jewelry.

It costs them just as much as it does the pros to live on the tour—about $400 a week, including air fare, food and lodgings, not including entertainment.

"I want you to put down one important item," Gerry said, leaning over the table toward the microphone. "Most women who follow the tour pay their own way. There are some who look for gratuities, but most of the fellas can't afford to keep them. This is not a sport for prostitutes. Even with the top players—they're either family men, true-blue, or they get it for free. Why should they pay?

"Most of the women I know often buy drinks and dinners for the ones who are not doing so well."

Those women also, they told me, assume different roles and become different characters for some of the pros.

"You see, most pros come from extremely sheltered backgrounds," Gerry said. "Playing sports has consumed them from the time they were able to pick up a ball, until now when they're hitting it. You'll notice that most of them are from the South and Midwest, some from California, and they've been brought up in conservative middle or upper middleclass families. They've missed a lot. The women fill in some of the gaps.

"Most of the fellows out here are really grown-up boys."

Unlike men in other occupations who after work meet with friends or lovers with other occupations; the golfer meets with his peers.

"They live in a bubble," Gerry told me, "a moveable one that bounces from one place to the next, all year long.

"The women become diversions for them, and they actually provide a short but sweet glimpse of the outside world. The women on the tour—wives, girl friends—have so little to offer in the way of worldliness.

"Mothers, that is precisely what some of them are. They give a hand to the fellows not doing well. They give them encouragement as well as a little sex . . . "

Others are out for a good time. A few of them show no discrimination. "They'll sleep with anybody, just as long as he's playing the next day. We call them "Party Dolls." I don't like them, they have no sense of propriety. They flaunt themselves, their bodies, and all that.

"Some of the guys like that sort of thing, but believe it or not, their kind is dying out. The men are human, sure, but they also don't want the word to get around that they did this or that with this one or that one. And, let me assure you, the word does get around."

Gerry and Jean, unlike the Mothers who chase after the less successful ones, and the Party Dolls who simply chase, are only for the winners.

"There is something almost heroic about the last two or three holes. Like a race horse, or even a track meet. The fellas have been out there for four or five hours in the sun. They've been hitting the ball with all the power and concentration they can muster. Every minute they're either lining up a shot, hitting one, or thinking about the next one. It's like playing a five-hour game of chess, but using your entire body.

"Even though they look tough when they tee off on eighteen, they're dead tired. The gallery gets them up, roots them on, but they are really bushed."

"And the tough thing," Jean interrupted, "is they don't know where they stand. They might hear from the gallery who's in with a 67 or what so-and-so is doing two holes back, but it's not like tennis or baseball where the guy knows what the score is. He can only play against himself.

"I get a real feeling the way they trudge along to the last green. I feel sorry for them sometimes when after they've gone through 71 holes they have no chance to catch the leader."

Gerry looked tired, almost as tired as her boy, Lanny Wadkins, who was still hitting irons on the practice tee. She made a ring around the top of her glass with an index finger. "I'll tell you something about golfers—golf pros—that I really like. They're more intelligent than people in other sports. Most of them have been to college. Golf is a minor sport in college, so they spend their time in economics, history, or philosophy.

"And another thing. They're simple. They don't have any of that big city, what would you call it, big city—"

"Hustle."

"That's right. When they talk to you they don't hand you their resumé in the first five minutes. You know—who they are, what they've done, what they have going for them. They're in touch with their emotions. When they talk to you there's part of them speaking from the inside, the soul, the heart, whatever."

"This sounds like a melodrama." Jean was sorry she said that from the look Gerry gave her.

Gerry leaned back. "Emotions. If something is bothering them they don't cover it up with how terrific they are. They tell you how they feel. I don't mean they cry on your shoulder, nothing like that, but if they do, so what? You don't get that from most men, do you?

"I was out with one of them in Miami. We spent the whole night in a booth on Miami Beach, in one of those restaurants. And nothing happened. Well, actually, a lot happened. He sat there and told me his life story, all the troubles he had, that sort of thing. But he also had a sense of humor. He could laugh at himself. He had a bad round that day. Not *really* a bad round. His score was all right; he just wasn't hitting the ball.

"I liked him very much, very much. He went off to his room alone, so did I. He was married. In many ways I didn't care. I spent one of the best nights with him that I've spent with any man. I think I've said too much, okay?"

They left ten minutes later.

It was Friday night and except for a few stragglers and the Burns Detective Agency guards, the grounds were empty.

Jean and Gerry, in their own game of winners and losers, face as much fierce competition off the course as the pros face on it. The women compete with one another for the pros as much as the pros go after the money.

The regular tour groupies have a common enemy. Regardless of their penchants for the winners, the losers, or any golf body, there is a group of women at each tournament that gives them loads of trouble—the volunteers.

Their function is to serve, which they do for free and with a willingness and dedication that rivals charity workers everywhere.

Many of them are young, beautiful girls with a fresh, outdoor look that reminds many of the golfers of back home, and many others of back at the motel room.

The majority of them are older, wives of club members, members themselves, career women who have taken a few days off to help. Some do not belong to the club where the tournament is held, but from other clubs, or no club at all. They want to be part of this grand occasion, and have worked long hours and many weeks preparing for the event.

There is a feeling of awe among them for the professionals, the officials, and the press people. After all, this is just one of many stops for these men. The volunteers feel that because the pros have been so many places that they are erudite, cosmopolitan individuals. They've seen more than most volunteers will ever see.

When the volunteers prepare for the tournament they hear things about the pros coming to their fair tourney. They have just come off five grueling days at some other club, sometimes thousands of miles away. Their names are perpetually in front of the public eye. Crowds follow them wherever they go, clamoring for their autographs. They are heroes.

There is also a kind of sensibility connecting the volunteers to the pros—the aura of the country club, America's cultural sports ground, where the upper class live and play.

I heard over and again, from the press tent to the links, that volunteers are the best action around. For one thing, there are no chances for reprisal. The girls, like sailors' lovers in every port, are one-shot deals. When the tournament is over, so is the affair.

The safety factor is also attractive. The woman would rather not let her husband or parents hear about her exploits. She will meet the pro in a room, and not in the night spots where she might be recognized.

The regular tour women are understandably unhappy. Barbara Ryder, who Gerry told me to see—"she'll talk but a lot of it is pure fabrication"—loathes the volunteers.

"They help out and that's wonderful, but I wish they'd leave the guys alone. First of all they don't know what he likes, we do. We've been with them more. Secondly, and I don't know how true this is, although I've heard of cases, the guys might pick up some disease from them that might knock them out of the tournament."

"Like what?"

"A broken leg." She winked.

Barbara was young, about twenty-five, and she herself was a volunteer at one of the Southern tournaments. She fell in love with one of the pros who has since dropped off the tour and is now a club pro in Alabama.

Her attitude toward the volunteers is similar to the regular caddies toward the local ones: they're amateurs in a game that requires professionals.

Her main claim to fame, she told me, was that she had been to bed with all but two of 1972's top ten money winners.

"Which two?"

"You wouldn't believe me."

"Try me."

She was right.

Before she took off for town she slammed one more group of women who she thought were "dangerous"—the townies, local girls who she said wanted only one thing: "To tell all their friends they slept with so-and-so. Just like a woman.

"Goodnight, Chris."

"Goodnight, Barbara."

6
The PGA: Potent, Glib, Absolute

"There's this fellow I know who works for Titleist," said my friend as we sat in the clubhouse. "The greatest guy you'll ever want to meet. I mean, he'll sponsor young kids on the tour, give players extra money if they're down and out. Everybody loves him. He loves everybody. Except one. The PGA."

"How come?" I wondered.

My friend shook his head, and gazing out the window toward the eighteenth green and beyond said through gritted teeth, "They think they're God."

He may be right.

In the beginning of American professional golf there was one power, the United States Golf Association. Charming, rich, eloquent, they owned the finest carriages in town and called the Ivy League their greatest learning experience. That was in 1894, when three chic eastern clubs and one from Chicago met to establish, interpret and enforce the Rules of Golf and to hold a national championship, the U.S. Open, which they still hold, but not much more.

Twenty-one U.S. Opens later, on January 16,1916, Ronald Wanamaker, of department-store fame, and a group of Eastern professionals met at New York City's Taplow Club to discuss the necessity of forming their own organization. Enter the PGA.

In 1968 a third party entered the scene. They too were eloquent men who wanted their own organization, but they had to stage a revolution to get it. The Tournament Players Division is still part of the PGA, but what started out as a wing of the outfit has since become the body that lords over the professional tour.

We hear so much about this triumverate that has made golf the thing it is today, but we've not heard much about what they do, or how they do it.

For three weeks every year Lynford Lardner, Wisconsin lawyer, a former state amateur champ and current USGA president, gathers his clan together to (1) determine the rules to use; (2) set limits on equipment to use; (3) say what kind of turf to play on; (4) remember the time they put the lid on big-time gambling in tournaments and clubs and (5) make a list of who is and who is not an amateur player.

For just $70 a year, payable to the USGA, anyone in the country can be eligible to qualify for the U.S. Amateur or Senior Amateur. You have to own a two-handicap or less to go after the U.S. Open.

The USGA also tells you the size ball you will use. It's at 1.66 inches right now, the result of a compromise between the British 1.62 and the American 1.68. It's been said that the British, not the USGA, did the compromising. The only one who seemed happy about the change was the organization itself. The ball manufacturers were less than ecstatic about having to make a new mold, and the players didn't like having to make the adjustment. On the docket now is a proposal to make the golf ball slower. The result, says the USGA, will be a shorter distance shot, which, logically, appears to make the courses longer. The ball manufacturers balk at this one because their biggest selling point is getting the long ball. The USGA is dismayed by the number of golfers who have been shattering par, but their solution, like the organization itself, is lounging in antiquity. Why hamper the equipment when the courses can be made more interesting tests of golf? But in fact, why beef up the course at all? The American golfer is getting better, and he likes it. He's got enough problems without giving him a couple extra strokes.

In 1971 the U.S.G.A. accumulated $1,478,275 to initiate and enforce rules like these. With a nonprofit tag awarded it by the IRS, it spent all but $63,576 on the championships, equipment research, turf development, and putting out publications.

In the midst of all this, the organization moved its headquarters from a New York City five-story brownstone to a palace on sixty-two lush acres in New Jersey's horsey Somerset County. The twenty-room nine-bathroom estate houses the best golf museum and most extensive golf library (6000 volumes) in the world.

More than transferring the books, the purpose behind the move was to lift the organization from its obscurity. In recent years the USGA had been worrying—not about a bad image, but rather no image at all. Within the first six months after relocating there were 10,000 visitors, about 8860 more than in the previous six months. The USGA has decided to remain in their strongest area as ruler of the amateur class and father to the nation's 12,000,000 weekend competitors.

In the years since Wanamaker and his boys established the PGA it has expanded in its world with the same remarkable results that IBM and IT&T have had in theirs. But there were growing pains. The first PGA Championship had the grand total of seven players. In the late twenties the first major conflict occurred: the organization was confronted by the disturbing fact that it was going in two directions at the same time. The first concerned the club members who sold the merchandise, taught the game, and organized local events; the other had to do with the professional tour itself. The PGA Championship was created for both the circuit and home pros, which meant the field wasn't always the best. Only members of the PGA could compete. Consequently, for a star like Arnold Palmer, who along with other young pros would have to wait five years to get his PGA card, the Championship was off limits. (It still takes a new player with no club experience four years to get his card.) In 1957 Palmer, who was third on the money list, was not allowed to participate. Just in the last few years has the Championship acquired all the top players.

When Johnny Miller stood before the microphones at the 1973 PGA and announced to the world that the organization had "tricked up the greens" at its *own tournament,* he was another in a long line of pros since the middle sixties who have not been afraid to buck the system. The first major hassle began with a feud between Frank Sinatra and Bob Hope. The tournaments, not the men.

In 1966 the PGA Executive Board informed the players' Tournament Committee that the $200,000 Frank Sinatra Open in Palm Springs, which had been already been scheduled, was out of the question. There is the Bob Hope in the same area, argued the board; two events would be impossible to support. The players, to whom $200,000 was (and still is) a lot of money, talked about not showing up for the PGA Championship later in the year. It was only talk, but more trouble started the following year.

Ever since television began covering golf tournaments in the early sixties the players felt they should get a piece of the TV rights money which had always found its way into the PGA's general fund. The pros wanted it for the Tournament Bureau fund, off limits to the parent outfit. No way, said the officials. The players persisted. They threatened to boycott the 1967 PGA Championship in Denver if their demands were not met. The two factions argued and promised lawsuits. With the thought of losing out on the purse money, for that tournament and later ones as well, the pros backed down and the event took place.

In 1968 all hell broke loose. When the PGA spiced up the standard entry forms with demands that the players give up a number of rights to the PGA, including all control over playing their own schedule, the revolt began. Gardner Dickinson, Doug Ford, Jack Nicklaus, and Frank Beard announced the formation of the American Professional Golfers (APG) consisting of players only. The PGA chiefs got very nervous. When, a short time later, the APG began work on forming their own tour for 1969 the situation became critical. Sponsors who the year before negotiated with the PGA switched over to the APG, and soon after the ABC network told PGA officials it would not televise their 1969 Championship if the top players were not there. The clincher came via a call from Dayton, where the event was supposed to take place. The city's chamber of commerce told the officials that if they could not guarantee the name pros, Dayton would also cancel.

Max Elbin, PGA president, wouldn't budge. The following November he was replaced by Leo Fraser, who knew a compromise had to be made. It was good timing on his part, for just a few days later, on December 1, Gardner Dickinson, the APG's first president, announced the creation of the APG tour—28 events and $3,500,000 in purses.

Some players wanted nothing further to do with the PGA and balked at compromising. Others, knowing the tour would be interrupted by further court battles, were willing to talk.

The APG had the PGA over a barrel, mostly because of all the big-name pros on the tour. Only Sam Snead sided with the establishment. Snead may have been a great player but he couldn't carry the tour all by himself. A settlement was finally reached, and the result was the formation of the Tournament Players Division, on whose board sat four touring pros, three PGA officials, and three independent businessmen. Shortly thereafter Joseph C. Dey, executive director of the USGA, was elected TPD commissioner.

Joe Dey has been called everything from "Mr. Golf" to a "great fellow" to an "insensitive big shot." He's all of them.

Dey had been involved in golf for forty-five of his sixty-six years, first as a sportswriter for the Philadelphia *Bulletin,* then as the conservative director of the USGA, and finally chief honcho of the professional tour. Before his retirement in March 1974, he ruled from the TPD offices facing Grand Central Station on New York's

Forty-second Street, a dozen blocks from Pete Rozell's football empire on Park Avenue and Bowie Kuhn's baseball dukedom in Rockefeller Plaza. The three of them, along with Clarence Campbell in hockey and basketball's Walter Kennedy, are the czars of the professional sports world.

What separates the TPD commissioner from the others has to do with the hired help—the players themselves. A Pete Rozelle can tell the player what to do after he's signed with a club. There is no such thing in pro golf; the players belong to no one but themselves. It is ironic that before Dey decided to retire he initiated what to many was the most controversial program in the history of the game.

I Know I Don't Own You, but Here's What You're Gonna Do . . .

"I don't think you're going to make a great tournament by making the players show up. The players will show up for great tournaments." This statement, made by touring pro Roy Pace, pretty well sums up the players' reaction to the new Super Tour.

Late summer, 1973. The TPD announced the creation of a plan calling for the appearance of the winners of the U.S. Open, PGA, and Masters of the previous five years, the current British Open champ, the leaders in TPD official standings for each of the last five years, members of the last-named Ryder Cup team, the 30 leaders in TPD exemption points of the last year and all winners of championship tournaments during the previous twelve months at 15 championship events in 1974. Which meant everybody who's anybody on the professional tour.

Each of the 15 events would carry a minimum $250,000 purse, making the Super Tour worth about $5,000,000 in total. A championship event in early September, which would include all winners of super tournaments, will eventually go as high as

$500,000. The current tour, with 47 events, totals $8,000,000. Under the new proposal that might be raised to $12,000,000.

The architect of the new plan is touring pro Deane Beman who replaced Joe Dey as TPD Commissioner in March 1974. Beman, thirty-five, has severed all business connections, including a partnership in an insurance brokerage, and has retired from tournament play to devote full time to the new job. He had an extra advantage over others considered for the job—tour experience. Before hitting the circuit he played for the University of Maryland from 1957 to 1960, took the British Amateur in 1959, the U.S. Amateur in 1960 and 1963, played on four Walker Cup teams and four U.S. squads in the World Amateur Team Championship. Beman turned pro in 1967. His tour victories include the 1969 Texas Open, the 1970 and 1971 Milwaukee Opens, the Quad Cities Open in 1972, and the 1973 Shrine-Robinson Classic. His career prize money is close to $400,000.

Along with friends, Beman also had enemies on the tour, a factor which critics of his appointment as commissioner say might incline him toward favoritism. On the plus side, however, was his siding with the dissenters during the 1968 revolt. And his refusal to join the PGA, which irritated officials, brought him closer to the players who are often unhappy with the Association. Those inside the TPD say what finally clinched the job for Beman was Jack Nicklaus' solid endorsement at the last minute.

When the 15 championship cities are taken care of, two dozen other events, called the Major Tour, will be played for a minimum purse of $125,000.

Sounds good, doesn't it? More money, fewer tournaments, more free time. Add to that the fact that golf would finally have its own Super Bowl. Dey put his own frosting on the cake by saying, "The 15-tournament idea would take golf closer to other scheduled sports. You expect to see Tom Seaver pitch in his regular turn and Wilt Chamberlain play."

Sounds *real* good. Wrong. Golfers, since they work only for themselves and not as members of a franchise, like their freedom.

Even Dey will admit that "all the leading golfers would be obliged to appear, and that's the rub. Pro golfers are like strolling musicians or troubadours; they don't want to be told when and where to play. They are the entrepreneurs."

Nicklaus, Palmer, and Trevino, as personalities with commitments off the course, will find it difficult to say they'll be at certain tour stops during the year. Foreign pros like Player and Crampton, if they are required to attend the big 15, might have to miss major tournaments in their native countries.

The reactions run the gambit. There are those like Lanny Wadkins ("Tell 'em I like it") and Lee Trevino ("Count me in") who will play enough and make money whatever happens. Many rabbits like it because it will mean more money for them on the Major Tour events that most top-flight pros will probably skip. Sam Snead doesn't care because he plays so little any more. Dave Hill, one of the most controversial tour members, says the TPD never cares what he thinks anyway.

The foreign element is universally unhappy with it. Gary Player will have to travel 15,000 miles a year from South Africa, something he will not do. "If it passes," says Player, "I will have to quit the American tour." Bruce Devlin is furious. "I am a free agent," he said. "Nobody can tell me when to play. I foot my own bills. The TPD doesn't pay my salary and there's no appearance money." Bruce Crampton pointed to the present rule which permits any foreign player to skip an American tournament when there's one at home. "This series format suggests that you must be seriously ill to be excused," says Crampton. "Something must be done, since I plan to continue playing some events overseas and don't plan on getting sick."

Then there are those pros with club commitments, like Bobby Nichols and Paul Harney, who attend only a few tournaments a year. Will Nichols have to give up his massive salary at Firestone to play?

Jack Nicklaus, without whom the tour would suffer greatly, says the TPD can schedule 15 events but only require him to play in, say, 12, or schedule 12 and make him play in nine. Nicklaus was one of the early pros to reject the plan, which irritated Deane Beman. Beman's reply to Nicklaus' alternative was this: "Our proposal is geared to having every star of the tour at every championship event. I won't buy anything else. If a player of Nicklaus' caliber refuses to sign up, I'm afraid his loss would be greater than ours. Nicklaus has a fantastic business operation, and it means a great deal for him to remain in the spotlight. I'm sure the spotlight will be on the championship series."

Blackmail, anyone?

Beman has backed down, though, and in early 1974 announced that three tournaments would be played the first year, gradually building to a maximum of ten. Leading players are required, in 1974, to play in the Colonial Open at Forth Worth, the Kemper Open in Charlotte, N.C., and the World Open at Pinehurst. Eligible players who refuse to enter the three events risk temporary or permanent suspension from the tour.

One of the biggest problems with the Super Tour will be confronted by a group the TPD has always bent over backward to protect—the sponsors. "The sponsors of championship events would have little trouble drumming up support," says Beman. "After all, they will have every top player in the bag. I think we will have an overflow of prospective sponsors for the series."

All tour sites will be chosen according to track records and the courses themselves. Sponsors who previously put on a good show will get the first nod. The courses, according to TPD's Joe Schwendeman, will be picked with regard to condition, layout, and whether or not the players have to use every club in their bag. "We look at the personality of every hole," says Schwendeman. "Does it have character? Take a course like Firestone, very long. Bobby Nichols the other day said he doesn't play it from the back tees because he's afraid he'll never get finished. Of course, Nichols is pretty damn long himself. But the length is not what makes Firestone great. There you have to use every club in the bag. We just don't want a course where you get up and beat the ball."

The TPD's original prime candidates were the Colonial, the Atlantic Classic, the American Gold Classic in Akron, the Glenn Campbell L.A. Open, the Sea Pines in Hilton Head, S.C., the USI in Sutton, Mass., Miami's Doral, and the Gleason Inverrary near Fort Lauderdale. They all have strong financing and are close to large metropolitan areas.

Some sponsors, who either have not been considered or have run into scheduling conflicts, have already taken action. Promoter Dick Heath has removed his Shrine-Robinson and St. Louis Children's Classic tournaments from the 1974 tour. Two other sponsors of events during the fall have threatened to cancel out if they didn't get earlier dates that don't conflict with the football games. And another said he'd take his out if he had to play opposite the British Open, which pulls most of the top U.S. pros.

What about the little guys who through twenty years of community effort have to turn their event into a big one? Take Greensboro. When the tournament started two decades ago it was as small as the town itself. The sponsors were the people themselves; they nurtured their tournament, imbued it with respectability, and made the course a championship one. Until now only a handful of other events got as much praise from the players or gave away as much purse money ($220,000 in 1974). Even though the course is not one of the more difficult on the tour, it's still one of the best run and most hospitable. If the Greensboro is not included in the Super Tour, and it doesn't look as if it will be, there's a good chance the sponsors will pull out.

Some players are worried. John Schlee says places like Greensboro, the Florida Citrus in Orlando, and the New Orleans Open cannot be expected to survive. Bob Goalby predicts that in a few years after the Major Tour sponsors are gone, all we'll have are 15 events on the circuit. Grier Jones doesn't like the new format because "the Pensacola, the Philadelphia, and the Orlando Citrus will not settle for being $125,000 tournaments, and I've just named three of the best. Just for being right nice to you and playing on good courses the $150,000 tournaments are the best."

The TPD feels it's taken care of the sponsor problem by having two tournament sponsors "alternate biennially in conducting a Championship Tournament and a Major Tournament; thus in 1975 Sponsor A might hold a Championship and Sponsor B a Major Tournament; in 1976, Sponsor A would hold a Major and Sponsor B a Championship Tournament." The fact remains, however, that many sponsors are worried about galleries not showing up because the name players are absent. Beman says they shouldn't worry and pointed to Arnold Palmer, who played in 25 events in 1972. What Beman forgot—or preferred not to mention—was that the PGA, Masters, and U.S. Open would not be included in the top 15, nor the Tournament of Champions, nor events with odd formats like the Hope and Crosby, nor Match Play Championship, which most of the big pros attend. Let's see, eight plus fifteen is twenty-three. The question is, where will Palmer play the other two?

What it all boils down to is that the TPD, like the PGA before it, is catering to the big-time sponsors. Financial disaster hit the Alcan event a few years back, the Dow Jones in 1971, and more recently, the 1973 World Open at Pinehurst. Bill Mauer, president of the Diamondhead Corporation, which put up $500,000 for the World Open, was less than pleased when Nicklaus, Trevino, Weiskopf, and John Miller failed to show up. Diamondhead and the other top-paying sponsors put some pressure on the TPD, saying in effect if the major pros could not be forced to attend, the corporations would pull out. Faced with that, Beman and Dey put their heads together and out came the Super Tour. Back in the nineteenth century British economist-philosopher John Stuart Mill presented to the world a theory called Utilitarianism, which states that the aim of any action is the largest possible balance of pleasure over pain or the greatest happiness of the greatest number of people. The TPD has instead chosen oligarchy, government by a minority elite. There has been a lot of talk among the players about the Revolt of '68.

There is one item on the proposal most pros like quite a bit—the TPD Championship. The first one is scheduled for Labor

Day week in Atlanta, with a purse of $250,000. In years to come the event will become golf's Super Bowl, in which winners of Super Tour championships will meet to determine who is the best. Some predict by 1980 the prize money will reach $1,000,000, which could make it sport's all-time big payoff.

The event was scheduled over Labor Day for a number of reasons. For most of the top players the season ends at that time; they have reached and passed their peaks during the hot summer months and usually spend the autumn at home or working on outside interests. The tour has traditionally been slow in the fall. In 1973, for instance, only ten of the regular 47 events took place between September and December; no purses (except the World Open) paid over $150,000; the Ryder and World Cups were played. Foreign competition is particularly strong during this period, and many American players do a lot of traveling.

The TPD Championship is the only real prize in the organization's package, but the players would like to see the event made up of winners from all regular tournaments as they now stand, without the Super and Major tags left on. *Just* the winners, and not all those exempt players, many of whom were victorious in the past but no longer. Whether there were forty-seven or three top finishers we would know that only the year's champions are there. One might argue that if Lee Trevino never won but came in second 28 times and was the current money leader, where would that leave him? Not at the Championship. If golf wants a Super Bowl like the other Super Bowls, where second place is not good enough, there can be none other than top finishers. If the Minnesota Vikings scored more and allowed fewer points but didn't win the division, or even the playoff, that'd be it. "To win isn't everything, it's the only thing," grumbled Lombardi. The difference between the winner and almost-winner (no matter how many seconds he takes) comes right down to that pressure and tension and drive on the last few holes. You either hang onto the lead or charge through the guys who have it. Lee Elder doesn't have it; otherwise he'd be in the Masters; Tommy Aaron, until his '73 win at Augusta, was the tour's best number-two man. In other sports, it's not how much money you've made or how many points your team has scored, but how many wins are in the column. That's what finally makes a champion.

What does the Tournament Players Division do for the tournament players? Not that much. "Our services to the players," said Joe Schwendeman, "are not that great or many. It's a membership organization. They pay dues of $100 a year. Now they get a little membership pin which allows them to get in and out of tournaments and they're eligible to qualify for the tournaments. I can't think of any other advantages. We don't have an insurance plan; the PGA itself takes care of that. Of course there's no pension plan since they're not employees."

In return for not doing much what control does the TPD expect to maintain? It governs operations of all professional and/or open tournaments and other events it sponsors, it oversees the conduct and responsibility of all players and sponsors, and it makes TV deals.

The events covered by the TPD are:

Opens. Co-sponsored tournaments for any exempt player or one who makes it through a qualifying round. Each player must pay a dollar application fee for each $1000 of the prize money, up to $50. The sponsor also receives $25 dues from each player who is not a fully paid-up member of TPD.

Invitationals. Co-sponsored tournaments whose participants are invited by the tournament's sponsor. At the end of play sponsors must pay not less than $5000 to the TPD for allowing them to hold the tournament. Non-TPD members must pay the sponsor $25 apiece in this event as well.

Major Tournaments. Defined as one having more than $100,000 in prize money. *Second Tour Tournaments* offer less than $100,000.

The Pro-Am. No more than 50 players can participate in each, and 75 percent of those must be exempt.

Exhibition Matches. No TPD member can participate in more

than three a year and those cannot be within two hundred miles of a regular tournament that's in play.

The TPD, along with the PGA, also enforces rules and penalizes the players for breaking them. Some rules are very unfair.

When Jim King allegedly tried to strangle a TPD official at the USI Classic he was not violating a rule of golf but of etiquette. It was called Unsportsmanlike Conduct, and King was booted off the tour. When Jane Blalock supposedly moved her ball on the green and was suspended for a year by the LPGA, the rule belonged to the game.

Charles Price tells the story of when Arnold Palmer hit a bad shot during the 1969 Masters. Palmer didn't get out of the sand and, with great irritation, took another swing—at the spot the ball *used* to be. TPD's Jack Tuthill rushed over and ruled that Palmer was at fault. Then four former USGA members overruled Tuthill. Five months later the USGA met in New York and agreed with their former members. Palmer broke no rule. He *did* break a rule . . . but he's Arnold Palmer. What if it had been Artie McNickle?

Then there's the card-signing rule. At the 1972 Greensboro, Gary Player forgot to sign his and went off to the locker, where he realized his mistake and went rushing back. Too bad, said the official, you're too late. The Great Masters Disaster of 1968 was the all-time worst when Tommy Aaron wrote a 4 instead of a 3 on Roberto de Vicenzo's scorecard which caused him to lose the tournament.

What about the rule that says a player can repair a ball mark but not a spike mark on the green? Lee Trevino wondered about that at the 1973 Inverrary when on the eighteenth hole his three-and-a-half-foot putt hit a spike mark and missed. "It's an unfair rule," said Trevino. "If you can repair a ball mark, why can't you repair a spike mark? Let's have one or the other. Repair them both or leave them all alone."

When South American Rogelio Gonzalez changed his score at the 1972 New Orleans Open, the TPD found out about it and told him he was through. Gonzalez made a mistake, he was punished, the end. Not the end. The TPD made a federal case out of the incident. Not only was (as Joe Dey called him) "Poor Rogelio" banned from the tour, he was made out to be one of the great criminals of the sports world. Dey said it needed announcing because the game was at stake. "The integrity of golf," he told Howard Cosell, "is all of golf. If you don't have that, it's no game at all." So what if poor Rogelio was sent into eternal shame and damnation? He'd spend it playing in South America.

One rule that had to be changed—slow play—is bringing good and bad results to the players. Back in the sixties, when Jack Nicklaus used to walk a hundred yards or more ahead of his ball to check the line, everybody did a slow burn. Jack was smart that way, though. The other players got rattled and lost the pace, which didn't help their score much. For Nicklaus, who had been doing it for years, it didn't hurt a bit.

Then when players started complaining and television wanted things speeded up, the penalties started coming in as officials in carts whipped back and forth across the course. Sometimes the officials get a little zealous in their duties. At the 1972 Heritage Classic when Gary Sanders and his group teed off on the twenty-fifth hole, one of the players lost his ball. An official warned them against slow playing. Fine, the player found the ball, and play got back to normal. But not the official; he'd found something to do and wasn't about to give up a chance to officiate. "The official was really on our backs good," recalls Sanders, who got so shaken by the harassment he finished bogey-bogey-double bogey-par and missed the 36-holes cut by one. "It destroyed me," he said. "Nothing like that ever happened to me as an amateur. I go four over par on the last four holes and miss the cut by one. I don't think I ever really recovered from that."

The official said he was only doing his job.

The final rule is an unwritten one which the players are calling on the USGA and PGA. It's called "Thou Shalt Not Trick up the Course." When Johnny Miller accused the PGA of tampering with the greens, the organization vehemently denied it. The truth is that tricking up courses is an old tried-and-true practice still going full tilt today.

One pro who's played them all, Grier Jones, says, "I think you will find the guys would like the U.S. courses a lot more if the USGA would leave them alone. And I will come right out and say this: I believe the USGA is the poorest course setter-upper there is. They ruin the golf course.

"They seem to think the greens have to be brick hard, watered in the front. It's like telling ball players in the World Series everything's too easy for you guys. We're gonna have a big fan out there and we're gonna blow dust in your eyes. That's exactly what they do. P.J. Boatrider and the USGA destroy golf courses."

Pebble Beach, which the pros love for its beauty but hate for the way its been changed for the tournament, is an example of the power of the USGA. When Jack Nicklaus wins with a one-over 289 and George Archer shoots an 88 on his home course, something's wrong. "That course is so ridiculous," says Jones, "it's just a joke."

The USGA has little tricks like letting the grass grow long in front of the green, and wetting the grass up front, so when a ball hits it stops dead. The rest of the green they leave hard as a rock and when a ball hits it usually goes over.

Take the 1973 U.S. Open at Oakmont and the 1972 at Marion. "You get to one of those places," says Jones, "and goddamn, they'll put in three new tees and two new bunkers and cut a new creek. If the course is so great, how come you're putting in all this stuff? Oh, well, they said, we were afraid you guys would chew it up. The players in the past didn't chew it up and they were supposed to be as good as we are. Has the equipment become that much better? The players feel the courses can stand on their own. The USGA doesn't."

The USGA likes to see the players tumble every now and then. Take a lesson, Bowie Kuhn. Plant rocks in the infield and watch the shortstop make six errors in a row.

7
The Masters
in Black and White

There are a lot of significant things about the Masters; one of them is that there's never been a black player or a white caddie.

But that piece of information is not high on most priority lists when the spring fever hits the pros who will be playing at Augusta National Golf Club. The Masters has an otherness about it, an aura not present at the U.S. Open and PGA, where electricity rather than charm prevails. If the three were films, award the Open and PGA an R rating and an Oscar for Most Madison Avenue American; give the Masters a G in documentary fiction and rename it "Civilization Refined, or Grits? We don't serve 'em."

Of the three, The Masters is the youngest, and also the oldest in many ways. Started in 1934, almost forty years after the Open and twenty after the PGA, it is no less then a magnificent occasion, the Mint Julep of the professional tour.

It's been said that the tournament holds court with no single tradition, neither old South nor conservative Republican nor closed-shop Reactionary, but rather has taken the best—or worst— from each and created its own.

Before one turns into the Augusta National grounds he must first travel through the town, which during Masters week is a mixture of antiquity and the latest thing. Inside the pillared, Georgian structures, Masterburgers with a side of fries go for $1.35 a clip; hats, belts, sweatshirts, caps, miniature golf bags, and little smocks, all shipped down from New York's garment district and all dyed green, the official tournament color, stare out at the street from their display windows; and elegant homes which rent for $300 a week during the rest of the year are now up to $2000.

On down the road and to the right sits Augusta National, its antebellum clubhouse, the magnolias, azaleas, and dogwood, and 6900 yards of golf course from the back tees.

Whoever coined the word "Masters" remains anonymous, but Bobby Jones, who preferred something else, has said, "I must admit that the name was rather born of immodesty." The 80 to 90 players who make up the field each year are by no means all masters. The old fellows are there talking about shots they made on such-and-such hole thirty years before. The traditional starters each year, Freddy McLoed, ninety, and Jock Hutchinson, eighty-eight, hit the first drives, which are then picked up by somebody else. Representing the foreign element are pros and amateurs, many of whom the average golf fan has never heard of. Half the field has no chance whatever of winning the tournament. The other half, however, includes the 15 or 20 best golfers in the world. They are the ones who inject life into the Masters each year.

The gallery members come from all over the world to watch the event and are seldom disappointed. Since 1965 when officials got tired of watching 40,000 galleryites (most of whom knew little about the game) tramp over the course, a new policy was initiated. Tickets are now by invitation only. Unless you know someone or someone knows you, the chances for attending the tournament are nil. "Everyone on the course, from the kitchen help to the players themselves," said one official, "is very familiar with golf." The pros universally agree that the galleries are the best on the tour. They are also convinced that the Masters is the premier tournament of the year.

Why, then, with all this excellence, has the Masters been taking so much flak during the last few years? It has mostly to do with the master-slave dichotomy still alive and well in the South. The first black man landed on Southern shores, and the people down there have been kicking him and themselves ever since.

For many, the Augusta National is still a plantation with the rest of the South as its fields. Those privileged few given the opportunity to work at the main house must do it as the help. All the cooks and waiters are black, the caddies and the maids, just about anybody whose function it is to serve. One rule stipulates that a caddie can't accompany a player anywhere without carrying his clubs; for a walk among the trees or down by the lake, wherever he goes. Another requires every staff member to have a security check that would rival the FBI's. It's not that the menbers don't trust them, but rather they don't want to *worry* about trusting them.

As far as the tournament is concerned: If the help is black and everybody else is white, which has always worked out just fine, what would be the point of upsetting that balance by allowing a black golfer to play? None, reasoned the officials, none at all. That was until a few years ago when racial discrimination took over the headlines.

Eeny, Meeny Miny Mo
We Don't Want No Black Pro

When the word "villain" comes up in context with black-white issues on the golf circuit, it is followed by "Masters." The first real scoundrel, however, was the PGA, itself no bastion of liberalism. The reason the PGA saw so few black pros before 1961 was because it legislated against them. Its constitution specifically stated that the tour was open to Caucasians only. In 1961 California's attorney general called the restriction a violation of state law and threatened to barricade all tournaments played on public courses if the PGA didn't reconsider. In November 1961, at the PGA national convention the Caucasion clause was scratched.

The Masters did not follow suit. For the next decade, during which two PGA co-sponsored events were won by black professionals, the people at Augusta did not budge. Colonel Homer Shields, a retired army officer, and New York investment banker Clifford Roberts ran—and still run—the event. *New York Times* sportswriter Red Smith tells the story of a newsman who visited Roberts one evening in New York. Roberts said he **had been** warned by certain people that if a Negro ever got into the **Masters** there would be no more tournament.

"If you think having a black man in the Masters would spell trouble," the newsman said, "try ignoring a black man who qualifies. Believe me, it would not remain a secret, and then you would learn what real trouble is like. For your own good, Cliff, if a black man qualifies, you invite him. In fact, see that he gets the first invitation."

Roberts has not had to confront the problem since no black pro has met any of the qualifications, which include: winning any PGA co-sponsored event; the top 24 in the previous Masters; top eight at the PGA and 16 at the Open; the British Open and U.S. Amateur champs. A black pro could have conceivably gotten in under Rule 13, which allows one player, not otherwise eligible, either amateur or professional, to be selected by ballot of the former Masters champions. That hasn't happened, but if Nicklaus and Palmer, who've won eight between them, got together and convinced a couple others, it would be a nice gesture and remove the stigma forever.

Cliff Roberts and his staff ran into their first major trouble in 1970. First, Lee Trevino refused to play in the tournament, saying the course was really not suited to his game. "It's just not my kind of course," he told the press. "With my game, I can't play there. They can invite me all they want, but I'm not going there anymore."

The PGA pressured Trevino into apologizing for his remarks and asked him to say his words were not intended as criticisms of the course or the tournament. The course did not suit his low line drive kind of game, but there was more. As a dark-skinned Mexican-American he wasn't treated with the greatest of hospitality around the area. Trevino refused again in 1974 for the same reasons.

The second problem involved Gary Player. After receiving threats to Player's life, Roberts assigned armed guards to protect him wherever he went. Right after that his caddie, who had carried his bag for years at Augusta, was forced to quit after being threatened by black activists. Player, who has been as responsible as any man for promoting integration in South Africa, was upset. Though outwardly he was congenial, the whole thing rattled him. It showed up in his score, which after two days left him six strokes behind the leader.

In 1971 and 1972 the furor increased. More threats were made, tighter security was placed around the course, but there were no catastrophes.

When the list of invitations came out in February 1973, the real trouble began. No blacks were on it because none had qualified. But there were still seven more tournaments to go until the Masters would begin, seven more shots to get in. One month later the issue became a national one. New Yorker Herman Badillo led 17 other congressmen into battle against Roberts, to whom they sent a telegram demanding that he invite a black professional.

No black is eligible, he explained to them.

That's not the point, they retorted, you've always practiced this discrimination. It's got to stop.

I want a Negro in as much as you do, Roberts told them.

Bullshit, replied the congressmen.

Into the middle of all this came the newspapers, accusing the legislators of bad-mouthing things they knew nothing about but admitting that—yes—the Masters has shown discrimination in the past, but that's all changed, and—no—you can't invite a player just because he's black. That would be reverse discrimination.

With Capitol Hill, the press, and Roberts locked in social combat, all fighting for the greater good, somewhere on the Inverrary course down in Florida, practicing up for the tournament, were the guys all of this was supposed to be about.

Pass the Three Iron, Amos

I've not yet mentioned the central characters by name in this drama because the black golfers themselves, as usual, have been given a back seat. For the congressmen, the press, and Mr. Roberts the *issue* took precedence over the man.

If they all thought back a few years, however, they would recall that two black golfers have actually won PGA events which would have made them eligible for the Masters. Charles Sifford did it in 1967 at the Hartford Open, and Pete Brown won the 1964 Waco Turner Open. But back then Roberts and company were not as open-minded as they are today.

There have been a lot of close calls since, expecially by Lee Elder, leader of the pack of black regulars—Sifford's cousin, Curtis; George Johnson and Charlie Owens, who switch back and forth between the satellites and the main tour; Cliff Brown, sponsored on the tour by The Supremes; and Jim Dent, a former caddie at the Masters.

Many are saying that Dent has as good a chance as Elder at being the first black in Augusta. Not only does he outhit everybody on the tour, including Nicklaus, his iron game is quickly improving. On the 1973 tour he won $26,393 for 97th place; in 1974 he promises to do much better. Dent came close to a win at the 1972 Disney World, but lost in a stretch drive to Nicklaus. One advantage he'll have if he ever gets to the Masters is having played the course before. On the last day before Augusta closes for the summer the caddies are allowed to play. He shot a 90, not bad for a sixteen-year-old kid on his first try at Augusta.

Lee Elder has had one of the great "almost" careers on the pro tour. It started back in 1967, his rookie year, when at the end of the American Golf Classic he found himself tied for the lead with Jack Nicklaus and Frank Beard. During the sudden-death playoff Beard was quickly eliminated, and Elder and Nicklaus had to go five holes before Jack sank a birdie putt for the win. Elder's second big playoff came at the 1972 Hartford Open. He and Trevino sank both an eighteen-foot putt and Lee's main chance for the Masters. In 1973 his streak again began up in the northeast, where at the USI Classic in Massachusetts (he finished second the year before) his catch-up golf was not good enough and again he came in second. The following week was the Sammy Davis Greater Hartford Open.

What better place than the first PGA co-sponsored tournament named after a black celebrity for Elder to make his play? But after two days of 66-67 he was still four shots out of the lead. Usually a quick starter and slow finisher, he made a switch comeback on the last two days, but the juice wasn't there and he finished in third spot.

There is an inordinate amount of pressure on the black pro who's in contention; the press hounds him constantly, asking him questions he's heard a hundred times before about his chances for a win and getting into the Masters. At the 1973 New Orleans Open, Elder shot an opening-round 65 to take the lead, despite the fact that the day before Badillo and his congressional cronies had sent the telegram to Cliff Roberts. More pressure.

NBC Monitor's Jim Kelly is a close friend of Elder and his wife, Rose, and spent time with them in New Orleans. "The sad thing as I see it," says Kelly, "is the amount of pressure put on a black player out here. Until we get a black in the Masters it will be very difficult, because every time you get a black player in contention or close to it, the press throws the obvious question to him

I saw it a year ago at Milwaukee when George Johnson almost won, and with Lee at New Orleans and Greensboro.

"I think really that the reason a black player doesn't get close to the Masters is because the press knocks him out. He gets so psyched up or so down on himself or so angry at the media that there's just too much pressure on him. It's really our fault."

When Kelly was covering the New Orleans tournament he said he had to apologetically ask Elder for an interview. "Obviously," says Kelly, "the black thing comes up and it is a story to a degree, but it's not the central issue in the second round of the tournament. There's still 36 holes to go and a lot can come up.

"I went into the locker room and Lee was sitting down there, and he saw me and he looked up and he looked back down, and he knew. Even though we're friends, he said, well, here we go again. I sat down and I put my hand on his knee and I said, 'Lee, you know I've got to have an interview with you; you're one of the stories.' And he just nodded his head again and never looked at me. And I said 'I'm purposely not going to bring up anything about racial stuff. All I want are the facts about the round, give me a key to the course.' I wanted a story on Lee Elder with nothing racial. He looked up at me and said, 'Are you serious?' He couldn't believe it."

If some players are used as vehicles for exposing discrimination, others have become the object of it. At the 1969 Greater Greensboro, gallery members screamed things like "Miss it, nigger" and "Blow it, nigger" at Charlie Sifford, who was so upset by it he missed the cut. Sifford, who along with a victory in the 1967 Hartford took the 1969 L.A. Open and 1971 Sea Pines, had received threats during the weeks previous to the Masters, which warned that if he won a tournament his life wasn't worth a damn.

Sports fans in general show little or no racial discrimination against black athletes on the field because the color barrier was broken years ago. It seems, though, that golf has the fewest blacks per capita of any sport. One of the reasons is economic; the young black cannot afford the equipment, hasn't the money for greens fees, and, for the most part, isn't allowed in private clubs, where most tour regulars get their training.

On the tour itself black players don't as a rule hang around with one another because there just aren't that many to hang around with. Knowing that most tour regulars are from the South, the average person would imagine a black player might have a rough time. It isn't so. Everyone is in the same situation of trying to make it on his own; the real team in golf is the entire tour itself, chipping and putting their way across the giant golf course they call America.

Whatever racial prejudice white pros bring with them to the tour is quickly dissipated when they meet Elder and company. "Hell, I admit I was brought up thinking I was better than Negroes," says one player on the circuit almost eight years, "and I know I haven't got rid of it, not all the way. But I know Lee and George Johnson, and I can see a lot of them in me. Like the need to win and things. Since I've known them the color of their skin doesn't matter any more. My wife says it's cause they look white now. I don't know if that's the case, but I like em. They're friends."

8
Over There

The pioneer spirit which says get as much as you can as quickly as you can, then build and build until you're the best has been one of America's driving forces since the country began. Whatever it happened to be, whether it was domestic or imported, Americans have always cashed in on it in a big way.

In sports, for instance, this country has borrowed bits and pieces and added a touch of its own ingenuity. Of all the major sports, basketball may be the only one completely home-grown. The rest of them have their roots in other countries; once absorbed, they've been pampered and nurtured until, when the time was right, they've filtered back to their places of origin. Revamped, renewed, remarkable.

Golf has been one of those surprise packages that, due to its success in America, has now become an international pastime.

In golf it's the U.S. vs. the Rest of the World: in players,

13,000,000 to 9,000,000; in courses, 12,000 to 9000; in equipment sales, professional golfers, and tournament purse money. But just as this country's golf boom is still pounding in our ears, loud rumblings are beginning to be heard throughout the world.

The idea for bringing the world closer together through golf belongs to American scholar and businessman John Jay Hopkins who in 1952 founded the International Golf Association, which a year later sponsored the Canadian Cup (later the World Cup).

The format was fairly simple; each golf-playing nation selected their two best players and sent them to the tournament for four days and seventy-two holes of golf. The first one took place at Beaconsfield Golf Club outside Montreal. Seven nations showed up: Canada, United States, Argentina, Germany, Mexico, Australia and a combined team from England and South Africa. U.S. Open champ Julius Boros and PGA winner Jim Turnesa felt, along with just about everyone else, that they'd win in a snap. They were wrong.

The Argentinians, Roberto de Vicenzo and Antonio Cerda, took teams honors, with de Vicenzo capturing the individual prize. The U.S. finished third from last.

The following year twenty-five nations were represented, with Australians Peter Thomson and Kel Nagle taking the honors. Sam Snead and Jimmy Demaret brought the American team closer; they took third.

Since that time the matches have taken on an international flavor, events being held in London, Paris, Madrid, Tokyo, Mexico City, and other major cities.

Fred Corcoran tells the zany story of the Indonesian team, Salim and Sjamsudin, at the 1959 event in Melbourne.

"Neither had ever worn a pair of spiked shoes. Each had only four clubs. Salim's equipment consisted of three woods and an iron. Sjamsudin had three irons and a putter. Neither had ever heard of Sam Snead. On his first shot, Salim sent his ball through a plate-glass window of the clubhouse. Sjamsudin, using a cricket grip, dribbled the ball only a few yards. Both shot rounds in the

90s. Wire service stories were written about the indomitable pair, who were honored at the presentation ceremonies with silver cigarette cases engraved, 'To the Players Who Tried the Hardest.' Clubs poured in to them from all over the world."

What started out as Hopkins' great idea has since become a not-so-great one, at least from an internal point of view. The World Cup has been taken over by five companies who have used the tournament to promote their enterprises under the guise of international goodwill. The prize money is incredibly low, but no player would refuse to participate, since his action would be taken as unpatriotic. The IGA might do well to seek out sponsors more interested in the game and the tournament and not as another big industry moneymaking scheme.

Others have picked up on Hopkins' idea and have suggested a world tour, in which matches would be played at various sites throughout the year. Australian Peter Thomson, five-time British Open winner and participant in most of the World Cup matches, was one of the first to advocate a tour of that nature.

There are drawbacks. One of the most often mentioned is, who will foot the bill for the players? In order to travel around the world, each player, at least in this country, where there is no government support, would have to be fairly well-off. Another problem is the PGA. Tournaments on the U.S. circuit would rather not chance the possibility of having a topflight pro decide to play in another country during the week of their own event. What, for instance, would happen if Player, Nicklaus, Palmer, Miller, and a couple others all went off to Spain during that week? the sponsors argue. A boring tournament? No gallery? No TV offers the next time? None of those things did happen at the 1974 Andy Williams San Diego Open when those players spent the week doing other things. But the PGA didn't say anything. What could it say? It doesn't own the players, though indications are that it thinks it does.

In an effort to discourage foreign sponsors from trying to get the world tour on the road, the PGA has said No! many times to players who have wanted to participate abroad, but it has done so under what might be called a blanket policy.

In 1971, for example, the John Player Tobacco Company of England sponsored a tournament that was giving away $150,000 to the winner. The company scheduled the event so that it fell the week after the British Open, thus enabling the Open participants to stay over a few extra days.

Folks at the Greater Milwaukee Open complained that many top players would remain in England and not attend their event. The PGA intervened and told the pros if they remained in England they would be in a lot of trouble. The John Player Classic went on anyway. The company was very unhappy, expecially since it was told to expect a few personalities. The company later withdrew its support of golf, deciding to keep its pounds behind its big money-maker, car racing.

Ironically, the Greater Milwaukee Open, according to the general tour consensus, is one of the worst. The course has characteristically been in bad shape, and the money is not so hot—even in 1974 it's only at $130,000. Add to it the fact that fewer than a third of the pros in England went to Milwaukee in 1971. The PGA, in exercising what little muscle it had, made two things clear: it was acting like a snot-nosed kid telling the world that—yes—it could tell the players what they could and could not do; and it also made it clear to the world that sponsors wishing to hold foreign tournaments had better make damned sure they check with the PGA first, which would entertain the matter, but they shouldn't expect too much.

The PGA has a special, built-in defense mechanism against reprisal from critics of the system. It lets the U.S. tour sponsors do the talking. PGA Tournament Player Division Executive Secretary Joe Schwendeman says this about the policy: "Say the tournament is in Japan, the pro will write a letter and say this Japanese man has offered a free trip for his wife and him, all expenses paid, and a guarantee, and everything he would win, and he'd like to take advantage of it because it was just offered for this one week. Can he be excused from this tournament? Well, most sponsors will go along. If it's the defending champion, we've got a problem. Or if it's Arnold Palmer, we've got a problem. But most of the other players get an excuse and then that player has to write to the Commissioner saying he'd like to be excused. Well, the way it works, if the Commissioner finds out from the sponsor that the sponsor has excused the player, then the Commissioner says yes, too. So, it's conceivable that the player can go overseas and not get in any trouble."

Conceivable?

"Let's say a rule was broken; how would the PGA punish him?"

"A fine."

Fine Jack Nicklaus? Fining Nicklaus $100—or $1000, or $10,000—is like stealing a bucket of sand from the beach.

"But now you get a young player who's scratching for every dollar, you fine him $100 and he's dying."

It's a lot easier—and safer—to squash an ant than an antelope.

It will be a long time before a world tour is established so long as the PGA and U.S. tournament sponsors have anything to say about it.

But there is a world tour, nothing as formal as what Peter Thomson and company envision, but one nonetheless. Fragmented, spread across two continents and half of another, it extends north to Sweden and south to Africa, from the Philippines east to the Iberian Peninsula. It has no single name, no official designation. Some call it the European Tour, which even geographically is not enough. Every so often an American will show his face at one of the stops, but he won't be seen again for a year or two. The regulars pick and choose their events, which are usually sandwiched in between trips to the beach, giving a few lessons or fixing their cars.

It all begins in late February of each year in Asia, where in recent years the tour has become very lucrative, especially in Japan, where the Sony people have dumped millions into the tournaments. Some of the stops include Pakistan, the Philippines, Singapore, Hong Kong and Sapporo, Japan, also famous for the Winter Olympics and its beer.

The Asian circuit, open to all pros and amateurs with a three handicap or less, has nine tournaments, with the minimum purse at $15,000. Four are offering over $25,000, and the Philippines Open gives away around $35,000. An additional prize is awarded by the San Miguel Corporation, also of beer fame. The company gives away $5000 to the top four performers on the tour. Among the most consistent entrants are Britain's Peter Townsend, Peter Thomson and David Graham of Australia, and Ramon Sota from Spain.

By this time it's late April and the pros move west to Iberia, where the temperatures are in the mid-70s. One thing the European Tour has in common with the American circuit is going where the weather is—the West Coast in the winter, Florida during the tourist season in spring, to the Midwest and North in late summer and fall, and on to the Coast and Florida again in late fall.

Many new faces appear in Iberia because the pros don't generally like to play in Asia, where the culture is so different from the European. The general feeling—more an excuse—is that there's not enough purse money in India and the Far East to warrant making the trip. The real reason is homesickness.

After the tournaments in Spain and Portugal, the circuit swings down to Italy for the Adriatic Open, and then on to the British tour during the summer heat. From Britain the pros migrate to Biarritz for the French Open, then back to Italy. The seven-month swing closes with the Italian, Swiss, Dutch, German, and Swedish Opens.

Golf in Europe is a strange animal indeed. First of all, there is not one public course on the Continent, and no professional makes his living exclusively from the tour itself. Ninety-eight percent of them teach at one of the courses owned by private clubs. They have to, since the majority of tour events seldom pay more than $2000 to the winner, and a lot less to those down the list. To add to the misery there is a lack of cooperation between the British PGA and the European Golf Federation, which organizes the tour stops on the Continent. Furthermore, the Federation has not made any significant attempts to line up additional sponsors for the tournaments, although in 1971 American Express put up prize money for Pro-Ams held prior to the major Opens. The final topper is that, outside of Britain, there is little or no TV coverage of the events.

No wonder golf has not been one of Europe's favorite sports. Some say it's the least favorite. All equipment, except for golf shoes, has to be imported, which makes the game a very expensive one. There are no more than 600 golf courses in all of Europe, many of which have only nine holes. For those who want to play behind the Iron Curtain, Czechoslovakia has two courses and Rumania has a private nine-holer. As a result no more than 130,000 people play golf in Europe, from Iceland to Greece.

Canada

Along with hockey and elements of basketball, golf in North America began in Canada, imported from England in 1873. Twelve years later the continent's first golf professional, W. F. Davis, arrived from the British Isles.

From that time to this, the game has advanced steadily, though not with the tenacity it's had in the U.S. Canada has been called the "five percenter" when compared to this country. The population up there is five percent of ours and the number of golfers, about 1,500,000, is about five percent of that in America.

What about professional golf? In the U.S. there are families of pro golfers—the Hills, Dave and Mike, and members of the Snead clan—but Canada takes the grand prize with Jules Huot, the patriarch of a family with no fewer than seven pros currently working the circuit in clubs or on the tour.

The Canadian pro circuit has been called a primer for the American tour, and rightly so, for the ten tournaments, while giving golfers an opportunity to get their games together, do not pay enough for them to survive. Except for the Canadian Open, which American pros usually win, the regular tour stops are provincial affairs, paying a combined purse total of no more than $150,000, hardly enough to live on.

The Canadian pros who have made it big enough to travel south—Al Balding, George Knudson, and Sandra Post on the women's circuit—have done well in the U.S.

Knudson was at the Hartford Open last year, where after two rounds of 67-66 he was two shots off the pace. His closing round 72 put him way out of the money. Poor finishes have cost him a lot of money in recent years.

Canada has Knudson as its only regular representative on the American circuit. Part of the reason is that the Canadian climate is not conducive to golf during most of the year. In order to become a professional a man has to have an inordinate amount of desire and stamina just to keep his game from falling apart. Knudson, for instance, caddied, worked in the pro shop, and won the Canadian Junior at sixteen, before hitting the tour.

To keep the game alive sponsors put up money for Bursary Tournaments, designed to give ten players under thirty enough money to compete on the regular tour up there. When Knudson began, the stipend was only $1500, not enough to live on, but his home course matched the sum. "You could live on $300 a week then, far from that now."

What finally made up his mind to travel on the U.S. tour was a win at the Coral Gables Open in 1961. "It's funny," he said, "but you'd think I'd do better in colder weather, especially since that's what I played in in Canada. Not at all. I prefer warm weather, to tell the truth. I don't have much meat on me, and if it's cold I just freeze up. That's why I play a lot of golf in South America, where I've had quite good success."

The younger players on the tour have made it difficult for him to keep up the pace. Knudson says, "The tour is much more competitive now than it used to be, and there are more good players. I don't think that the tops are any better today than they were ten or fifteen years ago, or any stage of the game as far as that goes. But the field as a group is much more talented and it is making money. A kid today has a choice between playing golf or going into law practice. Now he is more apt to give the tour a try. Look, the difference between first place and say 20th place fifteen years ago might have been ten shots. Now it's two shots. And this is what makes these kids so competitive."

For the time being, Knudson will be Canada's only successful representative on the U.S. tour. Because of the climate and the fact that most young Canadian golfers are brought up to be teaching rather than touring pros, the country will not make a major splash in the pro world for some time.

South Africa

In 1652, Jan van Riebeeck discovered the Cape of Good Hope and built a castle on it. Two and a quarter centuries later there was a meeting in that same castle. The subject: bringing golf to South Africa.

A few decades later Arthur D'Arcy (Bobby) Locke became South Africa's greatest golfer of the first part of the century, perhaps one of the greatest in the world. He was also the first foreign golfer to successfully challenge the Anerican tour. Sam Snead tells it this way: "Locke's famous U.S. invasion followed, and in five months he took $27,000 in prize money away from the PGA circuit players, me included. The boys were a long time forgiving me for encouraging Locke to visit the U.S. The late Clayton Heafner saw Locke putt once, and then bet Jimmy Demaret that Locke would beat Demaret and Ben Hogan in every tournament they played. Heafner kept Demaret broke all summer as Locke went from victory to victory."

The reason golf didn't take off like a shot in that country was that most Afrikanders considered it an English game, which they considered consorting with the enemy. All that changed in 1949 when Locke took the first of his four British Open wins.

Much more popular with his fellow countrymen than Locke —who was mostly English in his speech and bearing—is Gary Player, himself an Afrikander, speaking in his country's language and living there. Others who have made South Africa a country to reckon with are the Henning brothers—Harold and Allan—Denis Hutchinson, and Bobby Cole.

Though the country has no pro circuit, there are approximately 150,000 golfers—including many blacks—who play on 350 courses.

Russia

It has always been said that the capitalistic nature of golf ran contrary to the communistic inclinations of the U.S.S.R. Not anymore.

Plans to build the first golf course in Russia are being worked out by two American business tycoons, Armand Hammer, head of Occidental Petroleum, and Robert Dwyer, Sr., an Oregon lumber baron and member of the U.S.G.A. Executive Committee. The course is part of a deal Hammer's company has with Russia concerning an estimated $8-to-$10 billion to develop, with the Soviet government, Siberian oil and gas fields. The course will be part of a $125,000,000 trade center currently under construction in Moscow.

The idea behind building the course, aside from upping international relations, was to give visiting American businessmen a place to relax.

Some of the top names in American golf will have a hand in it: Arnold Palmer will be there for opening ceremonies; Robert Trent Jones, whose courses dot the American countryside, will design it for free. Hammer himself will put up more than $150,000 for the equipment, and Russian labor will do the work.

Though the course is billed as the first in Russia, it is not. The English constructed a small nine-hole layout a number of years ago, but it was plowed under by some irate Marxists who considered the course contrary to their ideals.

The greens will not be open to the general public, of course.

Australia

"Australian golf," remarked Peter Thomson, "has developed a maturity in the postwar years that has lifted the sport from the monopolistic pleasure of the few to the enthusiastic pastime of hundreds of thousands." How many thousands is difficult to estimate, but the sale of equipment over the last ten years makes it clear that the number of people who play as compared to the population is the highest in the world.

Australia's 1500-plus courses are always crammed. Five-hour waits for tee times are the rule rather than the exception. Jimmy Demaret once remarked that "Melbourne has more golf widows than any city in the world."

A professional golf circuit was started in 1947 and has since grown to ten events, including the Australian Open, PGA, the Dunlop International and the New South Wales Open, where last year American pro Ed Sneed beat out Aussie Bob Shearer for the $4500 first-place money.

Australian women have also come on in a big way. The Australian Ladies' Golf Union, begun in 1920, has close to 1500 club affiliates and represents 125,000 women golfers.

The Aussies have not only sent some of their best to the U.S. tour—Bruce Devlin and Bruce Crampton, and earlier Jim Ferrier and Kel Nagle—but they have been tearing up the European circuit.

David Graham and Peter Thomson have been doing it for years, but two young hotshots have taken the competition to the cleaners during the last year. Jack Newton and Graham Marsh, a hell-raiser and a math teacher, are the new breed from down under. Newton, young and blond, is known more for his playing off the course than on it. He has been called one of the most glamorous and controversial characters currently on the circuit.

Marsh, on the other hand, is a perfectionist. During the last year he has won the Scottish Open Championship and the Swiss, German, Indian, and Thailand Opens, but in the big ones like the

British Open, the Dunlop Masters, and the Piccadilly World Match-Play Championship (even though he reached the finals) he faltered under the pressure. That is what March and Newton are doing on the European circuit—getting experience. The general consensus is that Marsh will most likely not make a try for the U.S. tour, while Newton is sure to go.

The Bruces, Crampton and Devlin, are the Aussies' big guns on the American tour. Their combined money winnings over the years are fast approaching the $2,000,000 mark. In 1973, Crampton was in second place with $274,266, up from 14th place and $111,010 in 1972. Devlin was in eighth in 1972 with $119,768, though he played in only 21 events. In 1973 Devlin was out of the top 25, simply because he spends more than half his time designing golf courses with his partner, Bob Von Hagge.

Why has just about every Australian pro who has come to the U.S. done extremely well? Mike Hughes, executive sports editor for United Press International, who has spent the last seventeen years abroad writing on every sport imaginable, has his own theory: "The Australians are like the Americans; they're great competitors. Their country is bigger than ours, but they only have 12,000,000 to our 212,000,000 people, which makes their spirit even bigger than ours in some ways.

"The land mass is bigger, and furthermore a small man often is very aggressive because he's small. He wants to prove he can stand up with the big guys. The Australians are very conscious of the fact that they are a big country but very underpopulated. And nobody ever gets to their country. Nobody competes there—in golf, or tennis. I mean, the Australian Open is supposed to be one of the biggest tennis tournaments in the world. Last year—every year—everyone passes it over."

Another reason most golfers bypass Australia is the purse money. The 1973 Qantas Open, for example, gave away about $6000 to the winner. What pro in his right mind would fly all the way there and take a chance on spending two or three times what he might win on travel alone?

Some big pros have contracts there, like Jack Nicklaus and

Tom Weiskopf, winner of the '73 British Open, out of which a British manufacturer signed him to push his product around the Commonwealth. Weiskopf will probably travel to Hong Kong, Japan, South Africa, wherever the stuff is sold. England's golf-equipment outfits have a lock on the European market. Tom should make $2,500,000 over the next five years from his Open win. But for others the road to Australia is not paved with foreign-money.

"They get mad at this," says Hughes. "They think they have the world's greatest country, and *I* think it's one of the greatest. Their sunshine. The weather is good, life is good. There's no pollution. But godammit, it is from here to nowhere. It takes thirty-six hours to fly, even in a jet. You can understand why they're so upset and why they're such competitors. Sydney alone, for example, has two-and-a-half-million people, which leaves a little over ten for the entire rest of the country. It's a little like America before the West was developed."

Australia, in most ways, is still in the pioneering stage. The country is like America in another way, especially in sports; it has developed and made good the killer instinct. South Africa has it, too. Both British Colonies at one time. What happened to Britain, and *its* killer instinct?

Great Britain

The British, famous for recording their history, have not been able to come up with the date when golf began. All that is known for certain is that students at Scotland's St. Andrew's University played the game early in the fifteenth century, and that in March of 1457 the Scottish Parliament at Edinburgh, concerned about the war with England, issued a decree which stated that all men between the ages of twelve and fifty must practice archery in the interest of national security, and that "futeball and golf be utterly cryed downe and not used."

Geoffrey Cousins, deputy-president of the British Association of Golf Writers, surmises, "If golf in 1457 was so common a pastime as to require government proscription, it was evidently being played by all classes, and must have been in existence for some time."

Fine, but who introduced it to Scotland? Some say it was the French game of *jeu de mail,* now called pell-mell and played by London socialites in the city's Pall Mall club district. Or it might have been the Dutch and their *koven,* played on ice or in a court-yard. Or perhaps it was once the Dutch game of *chloe,* a hockeylike cross-country sport. Still other historians say the Roman invaders brought it in via *paganica,* played with a curved stick and feather ball. And then of course, the Scots themselves, who refuse to give anyone credit but themselves.

The game has changed considerably since that time, and so have the players. The first great golfers of record were all brought together in 1860, the date of the first Open Championship, when Willie Park, of Musselburgh family fame, sent to defeat Tom Morris, the pro at the Prestwick Club. The game continued on, with names like Harry Vardon, James Braid, and John Henry Taylor showing up in the winner's circle. Britain was also famous for establishing the Cups—the Walker, Ryder, and Curtis.

The Ryder Cup is a series of informal matches held between professionals from Great Britain and the United States. Named after Samuel A. Ryder, a British seed merchant who made his money by packaging flower and vegetable seeds in penny envelopes, the tournament occurs every other year. Since 1963 the competition has been composed of four 18-hole foursomes in the morning and four in the afternoon of the first day, eight 18-hole single matches both the morning and afternoon of the second day, and a series of four-ball matches (one in which two play their better ball against the better ball of two other players) the third day, with one point for each of the 32 matches.

Despite the fact that the U.S. has won 17 of the 20 events, the Ryder Cup maintains a great deal more respectability and feeling of national representation than does the highly commercial World Cup.

Year	Site	Team	Points
1927	Worcester CC,	U.S.	9½
	Massachusetts	G.B.	2½
1929	Moortown, England	U.S.	5
		G.B.	7
1931	Scioto CC	U.S.	9
	Columbus, Ohio	G.B.	3
1933	Southport, England	U.S.	5½
		G.B.	6½
1935	Ridgewood CC	U.S.	9
	Ridgewood, N.J.	G.B.	3
1937	Southport, England	U.S.	8
		G.B.	4
1947	Portland CC	U.S.	11
	Portland, Oregon	G.B.	1
1949	Ganton Golf Course	U.S.	7
	Scarborough, England	G.B.	5
1951	Pinehurst CC	U.S.	9½
	Pinehurst, N.C.	G.B.	2½
1953	Wentworth, England	U.S.	6½
		G.B.	5½
1955	Thunderbird R&GC	U.S.	8
	Palm Springs, Calif.	G.B.	4
1957	Lindrick C.	G.B.	7
	Workshop, England	U.S.	4
1959	Eldorado CC	U.S.	8½
	Palm Desert, Calif.	G.B.	3½

Year	Site	Team	Points
1961	Lytham-St. Anne's GC	U.S.	14½
	Lancashire, England	G.B.	9½
1963	East Lake CC	U.S.	23
	Atlanta, Ga.	G.B.	9
1965	Royal Birkdale C.	U.S.	19½
	Southport, England	G.B.	12½
1967	Champions GC	U.S.	23½
	Houston, Texas	G.B.	8½
1969	Royal Birkdale GC	U.S.	16
	Southport, England	G.B.	16
1971	Old Warson CC	U.S.	18½
	St. Louis, Mo.	G.B.	13½
1973	Muirfield GL	U.S.	19
	Gullane, Scotland	G.B.	13

The Walker Cup is a match between the best amateur golfers from the United States and Great Britain. Begun in 1922 by George H. Walker, then president of the U.S.G.A., the contest is composed of four 18-hole foursomes in the morning and eight 18-hole singles in the afternoon on each of two days, with victory in the match earning one point. The matches are scheduled to precede or follow the amateur championships of the host country so players may compete in both the cup matches and the amateur championship. The U.S. has won 21 of the 23 matches.

Year	Site	Team	Points
1922	National Golf Links of	U.S.	8
	America. Southampton, N.Y.	G.B.	4
1923	St. Andrews, Scotland	U.S.	6
		G.B.	5

Year	Site	Team	Points
1924	Garden City Golf Club	U.S.	9
	Garden City, N.Y.	G.B.	3
1926	St. Andrews, Scotland	U.S.	6
		G.B.	5
1928	Chicago Golf Club	U.S.	11
	Wheaton, Illinois	G.B.	1
1930	Royal St. George Golf	U.S.	10
	Club, Sandwich, England	G.B.	2
1932	The Country Club	U.S.	8
	Brookline, Mass.	G.B.	1
1934	St. Andrews, Scotland	U.S.	9
		G.B.	2
1936	Pine Valley Golf Club	U.S.	9
	Clementon, N.J.	G.B.	0
1938	St. Andrews, Scotland	U.S.	4
		G.B.	7
1947	St. Andrews, Scotland	U.S.	8
		G.B.	4
1949	Winged Foot Golf Club	U.S.	10
	Mamaroneck, N. Y.	G.B.	2
1951	Birkdale CC	U.S.	6
	Southport, England	G.B.	3
1953	Kittansett Club	U.S.	9
	Marion, Mass.	G.B.	3
1955	St. Andrews, Scotland	U.S.	10
		G.B.	2
1957	Minikahda Club	U.S.	8
	Minneapolis	G.B.	3
1959	Muirfield, Scotland	U.S.	9
		G.B.	3
1961	Seattle CC	U.S.	11
	Seattle, Wash.	G.B.	1

Year	Site	Team	Points
1963	Turnberry GC	U.S.	12
	Alisa, Scotland	G.B.	8
1965	Baltimore, Md. CC	U.S.	11
		G.B.	11
1967	R. St. George's	U.S.	13
	Sandwich, England	G.B.	7
1969	Milwaukee CC	U.S.	10
	Milwaukee, Wis.	G.B.	8
1971	St. Andrews, Scotland	G.B.	13
		U.S.	11
1973	The Country Club	U.S.	14
	Brookline, Mass.	G.B.	10

The Curtis Cup is a series of matches between women amateurs from the United States and Great Britain. Started in the early twenties by Harriet and Margaret Curtis, both U.S. Amateur titleholders, it wasn't until 1932 that the official events began taking place. Since 1964 the competition has been composed of three 18-hole foursomes in the morning and six 18-hole singles in the afternoon of each day, with one point awarded for each match. The U.S. team has won 11 of the 17 matches.

Year	Site	Team	Points
1932	Wentworth Golf Club	U.S.	5½
	Wentworth, England	G.B.	3½
1934	Chevy Chase Club	U.S.	6½
	Chevy Chase, Maryland	G.B.	2½
1936	King's Course	U.S.	4½
	Gleneagles, Scotland	G.B.	4½
1938	Essex Country Club	U.S.	5½
	Manchester, Mass.	G.B.	3½

Year	*Site*	*Team*	*Points*
1948	Royal Birkdale Golf Club	U.S.	6½
	Birkdale, England	G.B.	2½
1950	CC of Buffalo	U.S.	7½
	Williamsville, N.Y.	G.B.	1½
1952	Links of Edinburgh	G.B.	5
	Muirfield, Scotland	U.S.	4
1954	Merion GC	U.S.	6
	Ardmore, Pa.	G.B.	3
1956	Prince's Course	G.B.	5
	Sandwich, England	U.S.	4
1958	Brae Burn, CC	G.B.	4½
	W. Newton, Mass.	U.S.	4½
1960	Lindrick Club	U.S.	6½
	Workshop, England	G.B.	2½
1962	Broadmoor GC	U.S.	8
	Colorado Spgs., Colo.	G.B.	1
1964	Royal Porthcawl GC	U.S.	10½
	Wales, G. Britain	G.B.	7½
1966	Cascades Cse.	U.S.	13
	Hot Springs, Va.	G.B.	5
1968	Royal County Down	U.S.	10½
	GC, N. Ireland	G.B.	7½
1970	Brae Burn, CC	U.S.	11½
	W. Newton, Mass.	G.B.	7½
1972	Western Gailes GC	U.S.	10
	Scotland	G.B.	8

The British Tour, the cream of the European circuit, until two years ago was offering only $30,000 per tournament, satellite money in the U.S. Thanks to John Jacobs, a Britisher and former

Ryder Cup player who has been beating the bushes over there for sponsors and come up with some heavy ones, the British events, which in 1970 offered a grand total of $450,000, are now closing in on $1,000,000.

The Killer Instinct

Britain, which gave golf to the world, is no longer giving any golfers to it because they refuse to develop the killer instinct.

There is no pat definition for it; but it could be seen a few years back in Palmer's face when he knew he had to get up and down and began to charge; it's there in Nicklaus' determination as he bulls through the field. Then there are the Young Turks—John Miller, Lanny Wadkins, Grier Jones, Jerry Heard, Ben Crenshaw. By the end of the first three tournaments of 1974, Miller had banked three first-place checks at $30,000 apiece. Closest to Miller on the 1974 tour—Grier Jones, Lanny Wadkins, Ben Crenshaw, and Jerry Heard, in that order.

They all seem to have resolved to win, almost willed it. And they have.

From South Africa, Gary Player has that same determination, and Crampton and Devlin. This is Mike Hughes talking: "Crampton is going to fall down dead before he lets you out of second best, even if he's playing badly. I defy you to bring Crampton in here now and tell him Weiskepf is a better player than he is. He'll probably get up and hit you. You can't psych him out of it. Those Australians are determined; they want to be the best. They want to be number one."

It doesn't come down to how many dollars they have at the end of each year; the bucks will be there. They want to be recognized as number one, by the writers and the public, the TV and the galleries. Call it a need for recognition because maybe they were neglected when they were kids, or perhaps they couldn't make it in other sports and golf gave them a real shot at the big time. Whatever it is, there's a driving force inside them, a big voice telling them to go after it. That's killer instinct.

"And that is what the British lack," said Hughes, "not only in golf, in everything they do in the world of sport—they have a good loser image."

Hughes says for him the number-one sport of all time is soccer. Wars have been fought over a match. The great Pelé draws more people and gets more money than any other athlete in the world. At the 1970 World Soccer Championship in Mexico, there was a live TV audience of 80,000,000. More people watched that than saw the first man land on the moon.

To illustrate what the killer instinct really is, and that if England tries, it can take it all, in 1963 the English National Team fired its soccer coach, a schoolmaster type, charming fellow, very polite, who treated his players with patience more than anything. He was replaced by a man named Al Ramsey of whom Hughes says, "This is the most difficult man it has ever been my experience to deal with. You ask him a question and he says 'fuck off' and slams the door. You try to get into his locker room and he'll have you arrested for bothering the players. But he instilled so much of the killer into his players they would walk through a brick wall for him."

In 1963 Al Ramsey gave notice to the world that three years later the English would take the world championship. A lot of people laughed. The English? Schoolboys in a man's world. For those three years the press shied away, mainly because they couldn't get to Ramsey or his players. When the time came, in 1966, the English team took the field and proceeded to mow down team after team, until at the end they found themselves right at the top.

Most of the better British golfers are not after fame or fortune; they would rather live comfortably on the $25,000 to $30,000 they earn each year picking up a victory or two on the European circuit. The top ones want enough points to make the Ryder Cup team, which they can earn with the victory and placing fairly high up in five other tournaments. It's relatively easy to do that since the competition is not so fierce. The $30,000 is plenty, since the standard of living is not nearly as high as it is in America and because they only have to pay ten percent of it in taxes.

There are plenty of excuses for the pros not competing on the American circuit. Peter Allis, for instance, a four-time Ryder Cup player who also has one of the smoothest games in the world, when asked why he doesn't go to America, replied, "Why should I? I play a few tournaments, take a few weeks off. I don't need the aggravation of qualifying in the PGA School or the Monday hassle or living in a strange country. There's too much pressure, too much of a hectic pace. I'm quite comfortable in this easy life I've got."

Another case is Brian Barnes, son-in-law of Max Faulkner, who was the last Englishman to win the British Open before Tony Jacklin did it in 1969. Faulkner was understandably upset that his countrymen couldn't win their own national title—only he and Jacklin did it since 1949—when he sat Barnes down one day and told him he would have to go out and play the American tour, "If only for your country. You'll get the experience over there to come back and win it."

When Barnes got over to the U.S. he felt an immediate terror. First, he was not used to scrambling on the course, which one must do to win. Neither did he like the pressure nor traveling hundreds of miles between each tournament site. He lasted two weeks, got homesick, and left.

Another of Britain's great hopes was Neil Coles, who tied for second with Johnny Miller in the 1973 British Open. Coles is a great competitor, an extremely gifted player, but he won't fly. Consequently he's never been interested in coming to America. When he traveled to St. Louis for the 1971 Ryder Cup matches he went by boat. As a result he missed two European tournaments, right when he was on a hot streak, and that irritated him. If he weren't representing his country at the Ryder Cup, a friend said he would have gone stark raving mad for having missed competing in the two events.

Tony Jacklin is one of the few Englishmen to make a splash on the U.S. circuit; he won the 1970 U.S. Open by seven strokes over Dave Hill and gave his fellow countrymen restored hope. It didn't last long.

He had been tearing up the European circuit for weeks before he showed up for the 1973 PGA, where he finished 17 strokes behind the winning Nicklaus. I asked him what the problem was, since just two weeks before he took the Swedish Open at Vulva by a wide margin.

"Well," he replied, "I took twenty-one sorry putts on the back nine. I felt like chopping off my hand."

"What's the problem?"

"You see"—he looked down at the ground—"I'm a big man in Europe right now. I have the same following that Palmer has over here. Every time I play they expect me to win or be up there. But here, I'm nothing. So, I won the U.S. Open . . . I'm not an American."

The point was well taken. His gallery at the PGA was small. People mostly ignored him. The press ignored him. All he did was sign a few autographs. He was right on the button when he said he wasn't a star in America. He's also very well off in England—he owns a $750,000 home, where he employs six full-time servants and drives around in a Rolls Royce. Why should he give all that up for a rent-a-car and Holiday Inn?

Jacklin and his peers, like most British pros, are technically very good golfers. They approach their games as a mechanic does his machine, forever greasing up the rusty parts. But one could hardly call their playing "inspired" on other than a stylistic level.

If British professionals are ever going to acquire the killer instinct, they will first have to be exposed to it on their own circuit. The European Tour will have to be made attractive to top players from other countries, mainly by offering bigger purses. For a model, sponsors might take a look at what happened to tennis in recent years. Ten years ago tennis was dominated by the U.S. and Australia; now, with bigger prize money, the pro circuit has been bolstered by the likes of Russia's Alex Metreveli, Romania's Ilie Natase and Chilean Jaime Fillol.

Mike Hughes agrees that more money is needed, but he also sees the British golf professional's problem as part of a larger one having to do with England's national conscience. "You see," he said, "the Briton by nature is a very placid character who wants to mind his own business and not get involved in any hassle. He curses his government for all the days that he had in going out and fighting wars and being the great person representing the Kingdom. He's no longer interested in that. What the average British guy wants from life is reflected in the golf pro."

Just as the Englishman is a master of the understatement, he is also a champion of the understated. To live comfortably is to live well for him. He is paid for the work he does, and everything else is cream, but only if he doesn't have to go after it.

The House of the Rising Golf Ball

If some people are bored by watching the PGA or Masters in this country, they would be flabbergasted at what's going on in Japan. Here, related by *Golf Magazine's* Lee Mueller, are comedian Jean Shepherd's words about the new phenomenon:

"The Japanese people will eventually become the world's dominant force in golf!

"It's amazing! Know what I saw on TV on a Saturday night in Tokyo? *Prime time?* In color? I saw a forty-five-minute program starring a Japanese golf professional who was demonstrating how to get out of a sand trap! Nothing but stop-action and the arrows and little dots, all very seriously commented upon. It was a serious, involved lesson.

"They're *studying* it. This is the way the Japanese approach everything. They spent eleven years studying sports cars before they built the Datsun 240Z, which is now dominant in the sports-car world. The day will come when Japanese golfers—and maybe Japanese golf equipment—will be dominant in the golf world.

"I'm not joking. How's this for an image? The Rising Sun coming up again, like a red balloon, only this time it's covered with little golf ball dimples. That's Japan."

History books say it all started back in 1903 when a group of British residents built the Rokko Golf Club, a modest nine-hole layout etched into the side of a mountain near Kobe. The Japanese didn't think much about the course. Just as well; it was built for the English anyway. Eleven years later the Tokyo Golf Club was constructed by and for Japanese, but the only ones who played it were introduced to the game while residents of the U.S. and England. Some interest was shown in 1930 when Joe Kirkwood and Walter Hagen visited the country. Thirty courses were built over the next few years, but when World War II broke out and most of them were taken over by the military, the interest ceased to exist. In 1948, the occupational forces reopened them, which caused a mild flutter. Nothing significant, though.

The real blast happened in 1957 at the World Cup (then the Canadian Cup) competition. Twenty-eight nations were represented at the Kasumigaseki Golf Club in Tokyo. For the Japanese who knew about it, it was just another sports event; fifty-eight men from around the globe chasing a little white ball for four days over 72 holes; hardly a gala occasion.

Each day the natives read about their team challenging for the lead, and each day a little more interest grew in their minds. When on the last day Torakichi (Pete) Nakamura holed a two-foot putt to make him and his partner, Koichi Ono, the world champions, Japan exploded. World champions, to the Japanese, meant their country was the best on earth. And by nine strokes over the Americans, who had all but dominated the event over the years. Golf quickly replaced baseball as the national pastime.

At the time Japan had fewer than a hundred courses, most of which were enjoyed by foreigners and the very rich.

Thirteen years and a lot of craziness later the country had 550 courses, with over 90 percent of them private, and a million people playing golf. In 1973 the number of courses expanded to 747, and estimates ran from 7,000,000 to 16,000,000 golfers trying to play on them. Those in the know calculate that by 1976 there will be at least 2000 courses and close to 20,000,000 players.

The question most people ask is where will it all go? There are already more than 100,000,000 people crowded into Japan's four main islands of Honshu, Hokkaido, Kyushu, and Shikoku, all of which cover only 143,000 square miles—about the size of Montana. Such things don't seem to bother the intrepid Japanese, though. They are the world's foremost believers in Where There's a Will, There's a Way.

When Japan's Internal Revenue Department published a list of the top one hundred money earners last year, it became clear that a lot of them made their yen from land development. Yet not in the flatlands, which the government had refused to give up for golf courses, but in the mountains, where 18-hole layouts have been erected on the slopes. Every so often the government relents, especially when a luminary like Jack Nicklaus enters the scene, as he has, to construct an exact replica of the Old St. Andrews in Scotland.

The entrepreneurs who have not been able to grab up land out in the countryside chose instead to take their wisdom into the cities, where the vast majority of golfers live. There are currently over 5000 driving ranges in the country, 653 in Tokyo alone. From a distance they look like strange triple-decker birthday cakes, with all sorts of movement going on inside the layers and a constant flow of little white objects being spit out. So far there have been no reports of anyone falling off the upper tiers.

"What a way to die," remarked one man who recently returned from a business trip, "falling off the top tier to certain death, and getting pelted with golf balls all the way down."

The man who gave the ranges to the Japanese is Tokusaboru Sawai, the Mr. Golf of Japan, as he's known to his countrymen. He invented the triple-deckers sixteen years ago, just after the

World Cup. Sawai's driving range in Shiba Park charges $3.60 for a tee reservation, or for those who are willing to stand in line for a few hours, only $2.40. An average of 9500 people use the range every week.

The incredible thing about the vast majority of men, women, and children who make their weekly pilgrimage to the range is that they have never played real golf, out there on the course. Their experience has been—and will most likely always be if they remain in Japan—limited to whacking gnarled, sliced-up balls with range clubs—or club, depending upon what the supply is—that the sleaziest course in America would not even rent to its patrons.

But they love it. It makes little difference that the dull thud they hear when the club hits the ball gets them no more than a hundred yards; nor do they care if they find themselves on the third tier hitting balloon balls. In fact, as one man put it, there's a distinct advantage to the three tiers: "It's like a golf course, sort of. Each level gives you a different perspective. It's flat on the bottom, or you can pretend you're on an elevated tee on the higher ones."

In a way, the driving-range boom in Japan is not that different from the miniature-golf craze that hit this country a few years ago, except for one thing—the intensity with which they're going about it.

For those men and corporations who didn't get in on the bottom floor and start building in their own country when the golf boom hit, there is still the rest of the world. The Japanese industrial state has always been famous for its business acumen. What they can't produce in their own nation they hunt around for in other countries. Why tear down and make over what is already perfectly fine? has been their credo. One of their prime targets: the foreign golf course.

In Hawaii, for instance, Dai-ichi Kanko Corporation bought the Makaha Inn and Country Club for $19,000,000 and immediately announced they would sell 3000 memberships to interested countrymen. Other Japanese companies have bought half interest in the Hawaii Country Club, and all of the Francis Ii Brown Country Club. On mainland America, on the West Coast, Marin County's Peacock Cap CC was sold in 1972 to Nitto Kogyo Ltd., and some Japanese banks are looking closely at spreads in New Jersey and New York.

Since the Japanese began their high-volume exportation of equipment to the U.S. and set up branch operations to handle it, the corporations have felt the need for recreation areas to keep their executives happy. Furthermore, tourist trade has expanded significantly enough to allow the travelers a taste of their own country while abroad. What better than a country club to fulfill that need?

The U.S. golfers should not fear waking up one day and finding their clubs taken over by the Japanese. The country's 11,000 courses are not in danger, since private membership determines whether or not to sell.

While in this country golf is no longer exclusively for the rich, in Japan it is. The Japanese are very status conscious, what with their new wealth, and to make sure everyone knows how well-off they are, when a man buys a new car he will also purchase a set of golf clubs to put in his trunk, even though he might not play the game.

For those golfers neither fortunate nor wealthy enough to have bought a membership in one of Japan's courses, the greens fees run about $25, which includes a girl caddie (90 percent of the caddies are women) who carries a little bag filled with dirt to replace divots, occasionally some rice, and maybe a box of fortune cookies.

Those people *with* memberships might just have made the best investment of their lives. It's been estimated that a man who picked up a membership five years ago can expect it to be worth fifty times as much by 1980.

There are no memberships to be had in the country at the

present time; that includes the courses already in existence, the 250-plus under construction and the 550-plus still in the planning stage. And even death will not open them up. Most courses will not allow a dead man's membership to pass to an unknown person—only to the next of kin.

The going rate for memberships was about $150 back in 1937. Today, they have what are called "stage" memberships. Let's say a man wants to use his land to build a course. He solicits people who would like to join and charges them as little as $1800. This is the "first-stage" membership. The man uses that money to begin construction. When the bulldozers roll in and the work begins, he goes into the "second-stage" memberships, sold for as little as $3500. When the course is just about completed, enter "third-stage" memberships, for between $5000 and $8000. When the course is finally completed, the "fourth-stage" memberships are sold for a minimum $10,000, and take off from there.

On the foreign market the rates are naturally higher. One of the backbones of promotional golf is our old friend who doesn't belong but would like to play. The Guest. Whoever pays for the guest—himself or the member who invites him—the fee starts at $50 per round. Not per day, per round.

"Foreign memberships" is another term for highway robbery, but there is no crime if the parties all agree, and they do. When the Dai-ichi Kanko Corporation bought the Makaka Inn, the word went back to Japan that each of the 3000 available memberships would go for $25,000 apiece. The quota has been met.

The membership is only the first step in getting to the course. The second is what is needed when the golfer steps up to the first tee. Equipment. A set of golf clubs costs an average of $650. Then the player must buy shoes, balls, tees, a bag, head covers, putter, and a golf glove.

As if equipment, memberships, and range prices are not high enough, in 1972 Japan announced it would hold the world's most expensive tournament, the $300,000 Pacific Club Masters, won by

Gary Brewer. It looked as if Japan might not come through again in 1973, but Masashi (Jumbo) Ozaki tied American pro Bert Yancey on the 72nd hole and then went on to beat him in a three-hole playoff. Jumbo got $65,000 for the win; Bert walked away with $32,500.

What was it Jean Shepherd said, something about Japan becoming the world's dominant force in golf?

9
The Bagman

The Cisco Kid and Pancho. Batman and Robin. Don Quixote and Sancho Panza. The great teams of the world. Muhammed Ali and Angelo Dundee. Jackie Stewart and Andy Granatelli. The pro and his caddie.

If there is any teamwork in golf it exists between the two guys lumbering down the fairway. One bright and flashy, head down, white Foot Joys pumping one after the other; the other stoop shouldered, lugging a huge tournament bag over his back, Chinese-like, a few steps behind.

The dictionary definition of caddie comes from the Scots: "One that waits about for odd jobs." Nathaniel (Ironman) Avery, Arnold Palmer's caddie in his four Masters victories, puts it this way: "We work as a team—I hand him the clubs and he makes the shots."

The caddie's life on the tour differs from the pro's in only one way—he doesn't play. They both eat the same food, but not usually in the same place. While the player chows down at a Steak and Brew, his caddie gobbles a dinner at MacDonald's. The player will later sleep at a Holiday Inn; the caddie will be down the road a mile or so at the Breezy Gulf Motel with a "Free TV," black and white, a bathroom down the hall and five-year-old bedspreads that may or may not have been cleaned in the last few months. No matter, he'll be there only a week; or less, if his pro doesn't make the cut.

Like the players themselves who must rise through the ranks, the caddie goes through an apprenticeship of his own. Most starting caddies have to play with the tour rabbits for a while in order to gain a reputation and hope to be picked up by a money winner.

There are currently 115 regular tour caddies carrying bags over the winter months and about 60 during the summer, when the vacancies are filled by school kids on their vacation. More than half the regulars are blacks who grew up in the South; the white caddies generally come from the Southwest. There is little or no prejudice between the white pros and their black toters, even though the majority of golfers come from states which have just recently lost some of their bigotry.

More than 90 percent of the regulars have not gone beyond high school, 60 percent of those have not finished. Their attitude toward school is reflected by Jerry Pruitt, who carries Lanny Wadkins' bag. "I graduated from high school, but what's college going to do for me? I'd rather be out here associating with very wealthy people." Pruitt, at twenty-two, has done well so far; in addition to being hooked up with a top money winner, some offers have come his way. He's already turned down two $20,000-a-year club pro jobs. "The only reason I said no is because they're in hillbilly towns and I don't like Texas."

Pruitt started on the tour caddying for rabbits. His first start was the 1969 San Francisco Open, and from there he moved from one pro to the next until he got his big break at the 1972 Sahara, where Wadkins nipped Arnold Palmer by a stroke for the win.

Wadkins was looking for a caddy. Pruitt got the word that the guy Wadkins had in mind was being drafted, so he went up to the young pro. "Meet me in Los Angeles," Wadkins told him, "and we'll see how things work out."

"He did all right in L.A.," Pruitt recalls. "The second week at Phoenix it worked when we finished second. He was pretty happy because there we were, one shot off the pace and down to the last couple of holes. I talked him out of two clubs. He was thinking four iron, and I said, no, no way. I talked him down to hitting a big six. He hit it and it landed three feet from the pin. He put all his confidence in me from then on."

From that point the two young blond guys, less than a year apart in age, hauled their short muscular bodies across the country. Wadkins and Pruitt won the Byron Nelson Classic where they birdied five of the last seven holes; took a solo second at the Kemper in Philadelphia; tied for second at the American Golf Classic; a third at Houston; and through the Westchester, where I ran into Pruitt, they had collected almost $140,000 for fifth place in the money standing. Not bad for two young newcomers.

There's a system within the caddie ranks called the "We-He." When a player makes a great shot the caddie says "We" did it; after a bad shot, "He" did it. Pro Jim Simon's caddie, Paul Slagle, wrote a piece for *Golf Digest* about Creamy Carolyn and Angelo Argea, who haul Palmer's and Nicklaus' bags. "Creamy won the Bob Hope," wrote Slagle. "I know the papers said that Palmer won, ending a long drought, but as far as the caddies were concerned, Creamy beat Angelo, something that hadn't happened in a long time."

Creamy and Angelo are old timers in the caddie world. They, like the veteran pros, are getting edged out by the young ones. "When I came out here four years ago," says Pruitt, "three other guys and I were the only, what they called, 'long-haired hippies' at the time. Then we started slowly but surely, the younger guys taking away all the good bags. Most of the pros, especially the younger ones, all want younger guys because they're always dependable. A lot of the older ones out here drink a lot. Something is wrong with every one of these caddies out here, even me, you know? Something's the matter with us. We're crazy to live this life, but right now I just don't like to go home. I like traveling, I like seeing every week there's a different tournament, plus I like money. And I like to spend it.

"Some of the caddies out here are jealous because I picked up with Lanny. But that's the way the ball breaks. It's like fishing. You're there when the fish are there or you're not."

The caddie yard at any major tournament is where the action is. A lot of the conversation is about money, especially now that golf has become a huge financial success. The players make the big bucks, and the caddies want a piece of the cake. At the 1973 Westchester I went looking for a story in the caddie yard. There was one, sitting off to the side with a big grin on his face. He looked like the best bet, so I popped the question.

"Yeah," he said, "I got some of the juiciest stories you ever heard, man. I got some will blow your mind. Lemme ask you this . . ."

"What?"

"How much is it worth?"

"How much you want?" I asked him.

When I asked the caddie how much he wanted, the locusts moved in. What began as a one-on-one conversation became a symposium on cash. All the caddies had terrific stories, better than anyone else's. It took them about thirty seconds to forget about the money and another thirty to get entangled in a yelling match about who had the best poop and the most dirt and so on.

Here was a major coup; I was getting loads of information, and for free. Not so. There was so much "that ain't what happened" and "boolsheet" that after a few minutes I went looking for something more reliable.

A few years ago the average caddie was on the "ten-and-three" system, $10 a day and three percent of the pro's winnings. It's gone up since then, but not by much. The caddie still gets his three percent, but his pay has climbed to a flat $100 a week. Some pros like Grier Jones pays his caddie five percent of his winnings plus bonuses. Palmer guarantees Creamy $500 every time he tees it up at a tournament. A popular story about Palmer and Creamy concerns the time Palmer told his wife to write the caddie a check for $1500. His wife put an extra zero in, making it $15,000. Arnie supposedly made it good.

He probably did if The Baron had anything to say about it. In 1968, The Baron's last year as a caddie, he complained to the press that the pros were too damn tight with their money, pointing out that only Palmer and Nicklaus were giving them their due. He backed up his contention by saying a caddie is worth at least five strokes to any golfer, and he'd like to see any pro shoot a 66 without a good one. He made his comments at the Florida Citrus event in Orlando. The next day The Baron was looking for another job.

He was referring to such self-acclaimed tightwads as Frank Beard and Charles Coody, who feel the caddie is overpaid as it is. Since they don't want their caddies to do anything but carry bags they can't see paying them much more than slave wages.

Other pros like Chi Chi Rodriguez and Doug Sanders, both former caddies themselves, understand the value of a good one and that he's got to live well to perform well. When Chi Chi won the 1973 Greensboro he treated all the caddies to a steak dinner.

The younger pros are usually more generous than the older ones; when they came on the tour the prize money was already in six figures per tournament. The players who entered in the late fifties and early sixties found themselves in a lower bracket. The thought hasn't left them. They can't quite believe it when checks for $50,000 are passed out; and even though they see it all around them, they refuse to believe the cost of hired help has gone up that much. The caddie is the first to feel the brunt.

Kermit Zarley pays in the middle range, but he gives each of his caddies a little something extra. After every tournament, Zarley, a devoutly religious man, hands out a Bible.

Chi Chi Rodriguez' caddie is also his valet and bookkeeper. Dan Sikes' man tells him every club to use and lines up all his putts. Larry Hinson's carries a penny in his ear with the date he wants his boss to shoot. One caddie gets down on his knees and prays for a good shot; another wears the same clothes he had on the last time his pro shot a great round.

The caddie's major duties are keeping the clubs clean, checking yardages and pin placements and trying to keep the pro in a good frame of mind.

When he gets to the next tournament site, either by bus or plane, he goes out to the course to get the yardage. He'll pick out a reference object—tree or sprinkler head—and write the information on his note pad. Some caddies are more elaborate and draw pictures of both the fairway and the green, with all the markers and any other mental notations they might come up with. One caddie who's carried Steve Reid's bag used plastic overlays, a la military-map style, and would mark off each hole in half yards.

Getting pin placements was said to have been started about eight years ago by Jack Nicklaus, who was tired of wondering how close he'd be. He wanted to *know*. The ritual begins the night before or the morning of each tournament day. Twenty caddies at a time march out to the course, while one of them, usually a leader like Creamy or Angelo, walks up to the green and calls off the feet from the pin to the front of the green or to a trap. In the past, some of them would get lazy and wait back on the fairway for the information. Then the caddie on the green would march off the yardage to the pin and then about twenty to thirty feet beyond call off phony yardage. The next day when the pro hit a great shot but found himself either in the trap or over, he gave hell to the caddie, who wondered what happened.

Like the guy who is lost in some remote city but refuses to ask directions, some pros place no trust in the caddie. The players become their own caddies, checking yardage and pin placements. The only thing they don't do is carry the bag, and they'd probably do that if it weren't against the rules.

Another item they have no control over is gallery members taking off with their ball. Jerry Pruitt has had a lot of trouble with that when one of Wadkins' drives misses the fairway. "When Lanny hits his drive wide I have to run all the way down to the ball just to make sure nobody picks it up. In one round our ball disappeared four times. And then sometimes when Lanny's trying to putt he can see people walking around in the gallery. That disturbs him and he'll have to back away from it. So I sit there to make sure they stop. That happened three times today already."

One of the unwritten duties of a caddie is psyching up the player or calming him down. "There is a lot of feeling out there on the golf course between a caddie and a pro," says Kenneth Moore, who carries for Larry Hinson. "The pro gets so much feeling and drive from his caddie that he says, well, I want him. Like he's there for my spirit; he's good for my spirit!"

Moore is not one of those caddies the pro wants to keep his mouth shut. "I have to talk to him constantly," he says about Hinson, "to find out how tense he is. I have to watch his shots to see if he's tightening up. Say we got four or five holes to go and we got a two-shot lead. I ask him how he feels about the rest of the holes. He'll tell me maybe he's a little tired or his nerves are jangled. I cool him down. I mean he can get pumped up and still shoot a bad score, but, like, I took a lot of pressure off."

Pressure seemed to have gotten to Jerry Heard on the 1973 circuit. He placed in the previous year's top ten, but was in a six-month slump coming into Westchester. The general impression was that he listened to too many people about his game. The smart money said it was because his caddie left to get married. Heard's slump began that very week.

Take Johnny Miller, who has had the reverse effect. When his regular caddie was with Miller, he didn't play well. His top finishes were a first in the U.S. Open and a second in the British Open, both with club caddies. But he won't get rid of his regular boy. Four years is a long time to be with somebody, and Miller feels he has an obligation to his friend.

One of the big controversies on the tour concerns the local

versus the tour caddie. A lot of pros, especially Lee Trevino and Chi Chi, have been outspoken critics of the club caddie system. Prior to 1973 six tournaments refused to allow the pros to bring their own caddies. The Masters, U.S. and British Opens, the PGA, American Golf Classic and Western Open still hold the line. Only Westchester changed its mind in 1973 and gave tour caddies their approval.

Most pros prefer having their own, saying they know the players' game and attitude. Club caddies don't. Reliability is another difference, as many club caddies simply fail to show up on time, if at all. The regular caddie will always be there; he's got a big stake in his pro.

There are those who plain don't like the touring caddie, either because he expects too much money or, as Gene Sarazen tells it, he's dishonest. In an article published during the Masters, Sarazen called the tour regulars "gypsy caddies" who cheat and should therefore be banned.

"They sign contracts with the players for a percentage of the winnings," he writes. "With this much money at stake, what is to prevent a caddy from moving the ball or teeing it up to improve his lie?" In front of all those people, including the officials and marshals? C'mon, Gene. Sarazen's cry for honesty is a noble one, but his argument is completely unrealistic.

The battle among the caddies themselves has been in existence since the pro tour began.

The club caddies argue that they know the course better, so naturally they help the pro more than a regular who may never have seen the layout before. The tour regulars say that's ridiculous. They know their pros, what they can hit, how they're reacting, when to get him up and when to leave him alone.

"Local caddies think they know everything," says Pruitt. "They think they know the course so well it's unbelievable. They talk too much, all the time, telling the pros this and that, and they swear to God the putt's going to break this way but it doesn't, it goes straight."

The main problem with the club caddies is they work with

amateurs and not professionals; they are used to doling out tips
and yardage to the club members.

Another of the club carrier's big mistakes, one the tour regulars never commit, is picking up the ball. The caddie might think
it's already been marked on the green. The pro gets slapped with a
two-stroke penalty. A third misery for the player is exemplified by
one of the often-heard cries at the first tee: "Where the hell's my
caddie?" Another penalty.

Most pros want the local caddie to do nothing but carry the
bag and keep the clubs clean, but a lot of them can't even do that.
What happens is they get fired. "But you see," says Grier Jones,
who had good caddies at the Open and Masters and a fair one at
the PGA, "firing them can be a bad thing. You just don't want to
fire a kid because you're going to get his parents hot, you're going
to get the kid hot, and he's going to feel real bad about it. You don't
want to leave a bad impression on him. The clubs themselves ought
to take a little more pride in selecting caddies, then we wouldn't
have to fire them."

It may be sheer misery when a pro gets a bad caddie; it's also
treacherous when a caddie gets a bad pro. Most of the players the
caddies don't like are the cheap ones. Other pros are just downright
mean.

"I'll tell you one thing," says Pruitt, "I'll never caddie for
Arnold Palmer, I don't care how much he pays me!" He said it a
little loud and Lanny Wadkins, who was on the practice green just
a few feet away, looked up sharply with an expression that said,
What the hell are you telling him? It didn't bother Pruitt; he kept
right on going.

"He treats his caddie like dirt. Okay, I'm a caddie and I know
it's his prerogative, but I don't like to be treated like some lackey.
His caddie, Creamy, is treated like shit, gets stepped on every time
he does something wrong."

"Palmer's the only one?"

"Look, I'll caddy for just about anybody, but not Palmer or,
even worse, Jerry McGee. He's terrible. If one of them hits a bad

shot it's the caddie's fault. And they let everybody standing around know it's the caddie's fault. 'Creamy,' Palmer'll yell, 'get it together!' And he swears at him a lot. One time Creamy told Palmer he was a hundred eighty-four yards away. Palmer said he walked it himself and it was a hundred ninety-four. Well, they walked it off again and it was a hundred eighty-four. Palmer lied and Creamy caught him at it. Just because he hit that bad shot, he still had to throw the blame on his caddie. Is that fair? He can't let the gallery know he made a mistake. It would ruin his image. It's not his fault, it's his caddie's. It's always his caddie's fault. What are they looking for, a scapegoat?"

Still, the caddie is paid *not* to make mistakes and when he gets yelled at or given the silent treatment for a couple of holes after he's lined up a putt wrong, he understands why his pro is acting that way.

It was a Sunday, the last day of the Westchester Classic, when Jerry Pruitt sat near the putting green reflecting on the life of a caddie. Lanny Wadkins had just come off the first 18 and had another 18 to go because the rain wiped out an earlier round. He had just fired a 72 but was still psyched up.

"As we walked off the eighteenth, where he missed a six footer," Pruitt said, his mouth tightening up at the corners, "I walked up to him and said, 'C'mon, we'll get the next 18.' And he says 'All right!'

"I said we'll get 64 this time around, and it really got him up. I mean, both of us, we're both looking for that 64. And he can do it because he's super in the last rounds. He gets his charge going inside him. If he can make one putt, make a birdie on one of the first two holes, he'll make 64. I guarantee it.

"You know, it's those little things I say to him, the stuff you'd say to your girlfriend to let you know you love her. Just little things like that."

Wadkins walked over, squatted down and turned toward his caddie. "Ready?" he said with a wink and a smile. Pruitt jumped to his feet and hefted the bag over his shoulder. As Wadkins moved toward the tee, Pruitt turned back to me for a moment and said, "He likes to be behind going into the last stage. He likes to be two or three off the pace. I think we can do it, just put a good round on him. He's playing so damn good. We just gotta finish high. We gotta!"

10
Rabbit Stew

Farmington, Conn. Tuesday, August 28, 1973.

John Morgan, a twenty-five-year-old Canadian, has just come off eighteen and turned in a scorecard with nine threes written on it. "That's the best I've ever done," he exclaims. "I never shot such a low score before anywhere. It's the lowest of my life."

He has just been named co-winner, with little Butch Baird, of the qualifying round to determine who among the tour rabbits will play in the Sammy Davis-Hartford Open. The day is a scorcher —about eighty-five degrees—and so was Morgan's round of 65. But the only heat he's been feeling up to this point on the tour has come from pressure. The year is little more than half gone and he has pocketed under $1000 in official prize money. He needs $3000 to stay alive, to keep his playing card from being pulled by the PGA.

This is a big day for Morgan; he's beat out some top tour rookies like Andy North, who will end the year with close to

$50,000, and Don Iverson, who placed fifth at the PGA a couple of weeks back. Just maybe all the training, the ups and downs will finally pay off. It's been six years since he turned pro, two of them as a club pro and three on the Canadian circuit. This is his first try on the American tour, and suddenly, here at the Open, he's got a shot.

Hartford. Saturday, September 1.

John Morgan has just finished his second round on the Weathersfield course. He walks over to the leader board and sees that Jim Wiechers has the lead with 131, followed by Casper, Devlin, and Trevino. But those aren't the scores he's interested in; the real story is much further down the list at 140, the cutoff. Don Iverson made it, along with Frank Beard and Chi Chi Rodriguez.

Morgan pays off his caddie and heads for the parking lot. At the top of the path near the entrance he stops and turns back to the board where his name appears in those bold black letters: John Morgan: 143. He's had the feeling before, the gloom, that pit at the bottom of his stomach. The fear.

Vancouver, B.C. January 1, 1974.

While a lot of his buddies are in California trying to qualify for the Coast events, Morgan is thousands of miles away at home, wondering what to do. The PGA has his card, snow is falling, and the future is very dim.

On Monday afternoons throughout the year, when the big-name pros have not yet arrived and the tournament is cranking into gear, out on the course are about one hundred fifty rookies battling for a place in that tournament. The rabbits—Tony Lema named them that because, he says, they're always nibbling on lettuce since they can't afford steak—need to qualify in this one-shot deal. Twenty-nine will make it; the rest will pack their bags and move on to the next town, to try again next time. The definition of a rabbit is anyone who has to qualify. Some players are rabbits forever.

The percentage of rabbits who make it on the tour is low; the percentage who come to the realization that they'll never make it is high. It's one of the most frustrating experiences one can go through in his life; he's always so close yet so far away.

In order to get to the position of qualifying for the tour a young pro must go through an apprenticeship no less formidable than what any young man in the sport or business world must encounter.

The process begins early. It has to, for to achieve the discipline and make the shots that a tour golfer must have takes years of playing every day. Kids brought up in the north, for instance, are not as likely to succeed as southern ones are. The boys down south don't have to worry about the weather; they can play golf all year round. Over 80 percent of the pros now on the tour grew up south of the Mason-Dixon line.

Another factor is wealth, the more the better. It used to be in golf's golden age that most young guys who made the tour started off caddying at the local club. Not anymore. Grier Jones, one of the Young Turks on the pro circuit with over $300,000 in five years, says this: "Oh, I caddied a little for my dad, junk like that. My days were full. When I wasn't in school, I'd get up in the morning and play baseball, I swam and played golf in the afternoons. I just didn't have time to work." Grier's father, a geologist who made his money in oil, helped him out on the amateur circuit, where he'd have to excel to make it on the tour.

Lanny Wadkins is another one who had money behind him, a factor which enabled him to pick up invaluable experience—the National Amateur, the Walker Cup, and as an amateur on the tour. Family money paid the way. Take Ben Crenshaw who entered no fewer than 14 major tournaments as an amateur and missed the cut only twice. He even outscored Nicklaus and Palmer at the 1973 Masters. Nicklaus himself had a lot of national amateur experience. Wadkins, Jones, Crenshaw, Nicklaus, and many of the other top pros were nurtured on country-club living. Still, there are stories about the rags-to-riches pros like Snead and Trevino who, despite their poverty, managed to climb to the top. Those instances are few.

Dwaine Knight, who also qualified for the Sammy Davis but after a brilliant opening round 67, blew to a 74 the second day and missed the cut by one, is one of those rabbits who came from a less-than-opulent background. His story is typical of many rabbits on the tour. His father, an Air Force officer in charge of a missile plant, was an avid golfer. Dwaine caddied for him as a kid and started beating the old man and his friends when he was only fifteen. But like so many other tour regulars, golf was not Dwaine's first love. Baseball was. "It happened one day when I was running around second base," he recalled, "and you know how the straps went over the bag. Well, my foot caught in one of them and I pulled all the ligaments in my knee. One of my big assets in baseball was I was fast." End of baseball, and the beginning of golf.

Golf is a game that sort of "happened" to a lot of players. Hale Irwin was an All-Big Eight safety at Colorado; Jimmy Colbert rode in on a football scholarship to Kansas. Bunky Henry played at Georgia Tech and Dewitt Weaver was a one-time backup quarterback to Don Meredith. Grier Jones left baseball for golf: "I was good enough where I could play on the varsity in both sports, but they wouldn't let me play, so for some funny reason I chose golf. I guess it was the fact that I didn't have to have someone else to practice with."

Golf is neither a team sport nor one which requires an opponent. The only opposition is self, and for that reason the game is one of the most demanding in the world. It can also be one of the most rewarding. There is no one to rely on, no teammates to hold up your end if you fall. There's no Tug McGraw coming in from the bullpen when you've loaded the bases. On the other hand, in golf you don't have to worry about pulling someone out of a jam. You make it or break on your own merit.

Slide Rules and Seven Irons:
The College Scene

Frank Beard, known among other things for speaking his mind, made a ridiculous statement last summer: "I really feel there are some young men today wasting their time in college." Frank was talking about college stars like Crenshaw, then at Texas, and Gary Koch, of the University of Florida, who "are beating college rivals who really aren't in their class." Beard says they ought to quit school immediately and get out on the tour, where "they would get their brains beaten out for a while, but their games would progress much faster by learning from the best. You can get a college education anytime." Then, in his inimitable way, Beard destroys his whole argument with, "It's obvious players like Crenshaw and Koch are going to be professional golfers for the next twenty years." What's the rush, Frank?

In addition to the fact that they might be learning something in the classroom, college is the best training ground for young golfers. A look at the PGA tour roster bears that out. There are currently 124 touring pros who are former collegians, 87 of whom have degrees. And not as physical-education majors either. Topping the list are engineering and business students, then come liberal arts. The jocks are last. The University of Houston leads the way with sixteen touring pros, including fourteen who earned degrees. Oklahoma State is next with eight and Florida ranks third with six.

In the early days of collegiate competition, when the Eastern Seaboard dominated the game, Yale took most of the honors and still holds the records for number of team championships with 21 and individual championships with 13. As the country moved west so did the game. In recent years the South and West have taken over, especially at Houston which, since 1956, has taken 12 national championships.

Teaching at one of the southwest schools, Oklahoma State, is one of the most famous of all college golf coaches, Labron Harris, Sr. In his twenty-eight years there his teams have won 25 conference titles in 27 tries, the NCAA in 1963, have been in the top four at the NCAA 12 times, and in twenty-two of the last twenty-six years his teams have been in the nation's top ten.

Some call him the Vince Lombardi of the golf world, others have called Lombardi the Labron Harris of the football world. "Everything I ever did I wanted to be the best or I didn't play" is his philosophy, and by taking a look at some of the touring pros he's trained, it's understandable. Bob Dickson, former U.S. and British Amateur title holder and winner of close to $90,000 on the '73 tour; Jim Jamieson, World Cup player and Most Improved Golfer of the Year in 1972; Dave Eichelberger; Harris' son, Labron, Jr.; Jim Hardy; and Grier Jones.

Jones calls Harris his biggest influence. "He was a fighter and would never give up, and that's what he taught us. Winning isn't everything, it's the only thing." Harris expects his golfers to play at least five hours of golf a day, 300 days a year, which is the kind of training necessary to give a potential touring pro the edge over a rival without that kind of discipline.

Collegiate golf also makes one do what college in general tries to accomplish—think. The mental aspect of the game in recent years has fused with the technical. It's not simply the desire to win that makes good golfers, but the mental agility behind it as well. The ability to block out what isn't important, and to allow in only what is.

Most touring pros disagree with Beard's contention that the lack of competition is a solid reason for great college golfers to get out on the tour. Most players simply aren't ready the day after graduation. The real problem with going on tour prematurely is the pressure of making the cut, living on the day-to-day basis, and all the other afflictions that discourage a potentially great tour player from sticking it out. There are too many rabbits on the circuit right now who, after taking a dive a few times, have decided they're not equipped to handle that kind of living. When, really, if they got their games and heads together for a few months after school, and then decided to give it a try, the results might have been different.

For the young hotshot golfer just leaving the university, the choices must give him pause. His goal is golf's Jerusalem, the tour. He's dreamed about the place for years and has imagined himself galloping across its meadows on his way to stardom. The only question is how?

He could, as many have done, serve out an apprenticeship by working in a pro shop where he can accumulate enough credits to join the circuit, or he might spend some time on the smaller tours around the country to get some real-life experience, or he might go directly to the Tournament Players Division Qualifying School and win his Approved Player Card.

For the real comers like Ben Crenshaw and the Young Turk crowd, to whom the idea of selling golf gloves to hackers and wrapping grips on clubs in pro shops is out of the question, the qualifying school was the only route.

Before 1965 young hopefuls went to the tour on the recommendation of regional PGA officers who, though meaning well, often promoted their favorites over players who were better but didn't play up to the officers. That hardly seemed fair, so in 1965 the PGA decided to put the young golfers to a controlled test in what are now annual qualifying sessions. The 144-hole marathons are attended by golfers who have survived the regional tournaments. When the tallies are in, the top dozen or so scorers in each of the two annual meets are awarded their Approved Player Cards, which are no more than pieces of laminated plastic giving them the right to qualify on Mondays to play in the tournament the following Thursday. In addition to chasing their ball around the course at the qualifying school, each hopeful must pass a written examination on the rules and etiquette of the game, have a sponsor's guarantee that he'll put up a certain amount of money for the pro to live (about $15,000), furnish evidence that he has obtained personal liability insurance of at least $100,000 in case he becomes injured and another $300,000 covering each time an injury occurs.

According to TPD's Joe Schwendeman, the best TPD class was in 1969, when Bobby Cole, Tony Jacklin, Orville Moody, Bunky Henry, and Bob Murphy all qualified. Doug Olson, who was low qualifier, is still a rabbit, struggling along week after week. He was one of those who also failed to make the Monday cut up at Hartford.

Olson was a highly touted young player in 1969 when, in addition to winning the TPD School, he was also low scorer at his regional tournament. Things haven't worked out since that time. "I won both tour schools and immediately started playing poorly," he said. "I think I just lost my confidence. I threw my subconscious way off base and started changing. Consciously you just got to be worrying about scoring, your swing has got to be completely subconscious, you can't worry about it at all. That's how the great players play." Olson had always looked at his game from the technical angle, the physical execution of the shot over the mental. "I'm just beginning to understand the importance of the mental side right now."

Since the school began it's been an either-or situation for the low qualifiers. Either they've made it big like John Schlee, Bob Dickson, Grier Jones, and Bobby Cole, or they've not made it big like Harry Toscano, Bob Eastwood, and Bob Zender.

Perhaps Olson and the other unknowns might have waited before heading into the big time.

One of the brighter roads for young golfers opened up in spring, 1972. Known among other things as The Sweepstakes, the Down Under Circuit and the minitour, it is a novelty in the golf world. The Sweepstakes makes it possible for all the might-have-been and never-say-die players who have found tour going tough or have not qualified for the pro circuit to pick up pretty good money and keep their games in shape. The trick is that the participants bet on themselves.

Each player has to put up $7,000 for the 20-tour circuit. Each tournament covers 36 holes and the purses have run as high as $20,000, with as much as $6000 going to the winner. In return for the entry fee, the players are given food and lodgings and a chance to make a living. Gary McCord, who made a splash and then faded at the 1974 Crosby, won close to $90,000; Eddie Pearce, who took a second at the 1974 Hawaiian Open, won $45,000. Pearce missed qualifying at TPD School the first time. He said it was "a blessing. I had some maturing to do and also needed to learn how to play for money. Whether you're playing for a $6000 prize or $100,000, it makes little difference. If you're going to choke, you can choke for any amount. I now feel I can play for money and I'm much better prepared to take on the big boys."

There were high hopes when the Sweepstakes began in 1972. Glenn Peeples, a Tampa area pro who sponsored the first tour, pointed out advantages his operation had over the major circuit. No need for TV contracts, commercial sponsors, or even galleries.

He told *Sports Illustrated* in 1973 about the real beneficiary of the tour, the player himself. "There were 468 golfers attempting to qualify regionally for the PGA tour's qualifying school," he said, "but only 25 ultimately earned their cards. That leaves an awful lot of frustrated guys looking around for a place to play until they can try to qualify again a year later."

Peeples figured, and rightly so, that a lot of local backers throughout the country would gladly put money on a promising player in his area. When the first tournament rolled around, however, only 61 players were confirmed. But by the time the twenty weeks were over, 109 showed up. The results were so good that Peeples and his organization—The National Tournament Golf Association—predicted by 1974 the purses would run as high as $100,000, with $20,000 to the winners.

That's when the problems began. Sweepstakes tours began popping up all over the place; Valdosta and Decatur, Georgia; San Antonio and Austin, Texas; Anaheim, California; Grossinger, N.Y., and a dozen other locations around the country. The market became flooded. Twelve of them failed before the first tee shot was hit, and of the 17 that actually got started, only two currently exist. One of the casualties was in Southern California where Gene Littler, who attached his name to it, and the Golf Inns motel chain required entrants to put up a $680 fee for each tournament and play for a minimum $30,000 purse. It folded after six events.

The reasons for so many shutting down, in addition to the overcrowded market, are ones any business has to face when it tries to take too much in a hurry. Not enough golfers could hustle up backers; some tournament promoters promised purses and then didn't come up with them, irritating one golfer in Arizona enough to shoot the promoter there. The word got around that everything wasn't exactly aboveboard, so players and backers alike refused to put up money unless the promoter had already established himself. Few of them had.

TPD Commissioner Joe Dey predicted the demise of the Sweepstakes because of financial difficulties. He pointed specifically to the way the winnings were distributed—only twenty percent of those playing made any money. Glen Peeples disagrees. "In a way," says Peeples, "Joe Dey and his tour haven't taken care of the needs of golf. Too many fine players are shut out. There must be a better way. I can see outside sponsors like Buick or Pepsi-Cola becoming involved, so that the players put up less and less and play for more and more. I see telecasts of the tournaments each week. If the PGA would help out, I can see this as a logical way to qualify for the pro tour.

"But what I really see in the end is no pro tour at all, just three or four regionally oriented things going on simultaneously around the country, with top players setting out from time to time to meet in six or eight major championships. Don't you think something like that would appeal to even a Jack Nicklaus?"

The PGA has no official stance on the Sweepstakes. TPD's Joe Schwendeman says the only way for the PGA to get involved is "if one of our players went down and played in the thing and did not, prior to that, get an excuse from our schedule tournament sponsor." The PGA won't have to worry too much about that, since most of the Sweepstakes bar tournament players, some won't let any in who made $10,000 or more during the previous year on the tour, others won't allow any of the top-sixty money winners, and two of them refused to let players in with cards.

One regular tour member the Sweepstakes helped immensely was 1969 U.S. Open champ and World Series of Golf winner Orville Moody. Moody hit a major slump in 1972; it was so bad in fact that his total earnings for the year came to less than $14,000. At the beginning of 1973 he got excuses from the regular tour to compete in the Sweepstakes down in San Antonio, where his home is. He played for eight weeks and won close to $20,000.

"It really helped him," says Schwendeman. "His game was in pretty bad shape, and he was having trouble with his divorce. It helped him regain confidence, and he's been playing pretty well since he's been back. I mean he hasn't threatened, but it sure cleaned up his game."

It cleaned it up a lot. Moody hit an all-time high on the 1973 tour with 36th-place money of $74,286.

A further testimony to the advantages of the Sweepstakes is that 22 of the 25 members of the 1973 TPD graduating class sharpened up their games and purses on the tour. It looks as if Peeples is right when he says the Sweepstakes has become one of golf's permanent fixtures.

The easiest but the most time-consuming way for a player to get on the tour is the apprenticeship route. Working in a pro shop to accumulate enough credits for the tour is like hanging around purgatory. The wait can kill you. A young pro's game gets rusty, there are seldom any good players around, all but eliminating the competitive edge, and like a hugh, festering sore, the idea of security begins creeping up on him. There are hundreds of excellent golfers working pro shops who with a little push might have been on the tour today. But their time has passed. They've reconciled themselves to marrying a local girl, having a couple of kids and hoping the head pro will die or something so they can take over.

The assistant pro's world is filled with dreams and nagging questions that begin with "If I only . . . " and "What if . . . " Some day perhaps he'll turn into a good teaching pro showing geriatric hackers how to break their flat swing and occasionally running into a tour regular who's heard about him and wants a lesson or two. But haunting him always will be whether a few years ago he might have made it to the big time. An awful thought to carry to his grave.

Have I Got a Deal for You, Kid: The Sponsor

On March 16, 1973, rabbit Gary Sanders shot a second round 72 in the Greater Jacksonville Open and for the first time in 13 tournaments made the cut, which meant he was exempt from qualifying for the next tournament. He rushed back to the motel where he and his wife, Linda, had a giant celebration. In the middle of it all the phone rang. It was his sponsor, Milburn Industries, who told him he was dropped, no money, the end. Milburn had promised to give him $30,000 a year for two years in return for a share of his purses.

Sanders, with $33 to his name (not even enough to pay his caddie), in ecstasy a moment before, was suddenly thrown into deep depression. "It was the most total shock of my life," he recalled. "I thought the one thing I had was security and now it was gone. I had offers from a number of potential sponsors, but I signed with a big company to assure security. Now exactly what I thought could not happen had happened."

Milburn president Gene Eichler expressed his sympathy: "It had nothing to do with the way Gary was playing. Several of our projects went sour and we weren't able to continue backing him. We were struggling to stay alive financially at the time.

"We're all rooting for him and in no way were disappointed

in him. Quite the contrary, we've always felt he was going to make it and wish we could still be with him."

The spark taken out of him, Sanders shot a 77 the next day and a final 74 to win $295.87. It's called getting royally screwed.

Most sponsors are out for a fast buck; they see a kid who's hot, he's won a few amateur titles, the press likes him, and his father doesn't make enough money to support him on the tour. They come into the player's life waving checks in his face and offering him the best of all financial worlds. "Think about it, kid," they tell him. "With my money and your talent the sky's the limit." The kid, who knows his time is right, grabs for the bait and is hooked.

Sponsors have been notorious for taking young pros for a ride and then dropping them off in some remote place with no money and little chance to come up with some. Tour regulars Dwight Neville, Ben Curren, and Gibby Gilbert have been down that road. At least Milburn Industries had the decency to call Gary Sanders; other sponsors have simply stopped sending checks.

The contract between the pro and his backer usually states that the pro will pay the sponsors back with everything he wins until the initial investment is met. Then it's a fifty-fifty split, for God knows how long in some cases. This is called being locked in. Most court cases having to do with golf are those in which the pro is trying to shed his hungry backer. Say, for example, a pro spends four years and $100,000 of his backer's money, and all of a sudden he wins $30,000 in some tournament. Everybody says Wow!, but it all goes back in the sponsor's pocket.

Not all sponsors operate that way. Grier Jones' situation is ideal. His father, his wife's uncle, and three friends put up $20,000 on his first year. "They let me have everything I made off the tour," says Jones. "They took everything I made on it." Which means he got to keep anything he made from endorsements. It also means that the initial $20,000 the sponsors took back, and the next $20,000 they got half of. During the third year (1972) he asked to be a one-quarter sponsor, which was agreed upon. He became a half sponsor during 1973, with one added attraction. Before he could keep only endorsements; in 1973 he got to keep pro-am purses and any money he won overseas. "I was very lucky to have family behind me, my mind was always at ease."

Other sponsors who expect no money in return are the equipment and clothing manufacturers who have made a fortune by having the players use their stuff. Top pros like Nicklaus and Player not only receive free equipment, they also sign money contracts that often run into six figures. The rabbits, on the other hand, get clubs, a bag with the sponsor's name on it and two dozen new balls a week. The reason the two-dozen figure was chosen is because the sponsors don't expect the rookie to make the cut, and the most balls he can possibly use in two rounds are 24. If the rookie somehow does make it to the third day, there's usually a representative around who'll give him two dozen more. Wilson, Spaulding, Hogan, First Flight, and Titleist are the equipment people most in evidence, while Munsingwear, Izod, Jantzen and, oddly enough, Amana, grab the clothing honors. Amana has been hustling around for a few years trying to get pros to wear a hat with its name on it for $50 a week. Who should show up in the 1973 PGA tourbook wearing the hats? Bob Goalby and Miller Barber.

For the pros who have done better than most, the clothing companies will not only outfit the player but also his wife and kids. There have been few gripes against these companies, except occasionally by a pro who finds himself suddenly dropped because he's not been doing so well. Two of the most dependable manufacturers are MacGregor and Jantzen, who have been known to stand by the pros regardless of how they're doing.

The biggest concern for the players is the ball. Until two years ago the one most pros played was the Titleist; in fact, it's still the most popular but many players have dropped it because of the new design. The new larger dimples in the Titleist have made it unpredictable, something the pros can do without. Dwaine Knight puts it like this: "I like the old standard Titleist. Maybe I'm kind of conservative in that way, but at least I know where it's going, so I use it." Grier Jones agrees. "The new Titleist is not a good ball in the wind. There's too much variation. Sometimes it upshoots, then it drops down. I will never play their ball again until they come back with the old one."

Many tour regulars have made a switch to MacGregor's Tourney, including Nicklaus, Miller and Weiskopf because it *is* predictable.

Getting There: Life Off the Course

Golf is one sport not involved in the home game–away game syndrome of other sports. The only "home" for golfers may be a tournament played on a home course, but that seldom happens. Consequently, the pros remain nomads, trucking their clubs and reputations from one tour stop to another. Golf is not an indoor sport, which makes weather a major factor. There are no Astrodomes or field houses to keep the rain out. Nor is there a playing field with specific dimensions. A football field in Green Bay is the same size as one in Miami, a basketball court in New York has identical dimensions to one in Los Angeles.

From the waves pelting the shores of Pebble Beach to the flatlands of Miami's Doral to the hills of Firestone, each course is unique.

Golf is also different from other sports in that it's not seasonal. Play begins during the first week of January and ends in December. Furthermore, unlike in other sports, the ball is never touched while in play. When the golfer approaches his shot his ball is motionless, which essentially means he has to conjure up a lot more inner concentration than, say, a baseball player who reacts to the ball coming at him.

Some people refuse to call golf a sport because there's no running in the game. Part of their definition of a sport includes moving quickly. Obviously they have never felt the excitement of a closing charge, nor heard the scream of a gallery, nor experienced the intensity at the eighteenth hole.

Those sensations, plus the money, the atmosphere, the thrill of personal satisfaction, and the uncertainty of the game itself are what make the amateur golfer take the professional route. It's no easy thing for a young rookie out on his first tour. Before he hits the first tee shot he must have at least $15,000 in his pocket, just to get where he has to go.

The first month and a half of the 1973 travel schedule was not that difficult; if the pro decided to skip the Hawaiian Open, he remained on the West Coast. The big jump came in February when he took off across country to the Jackie Gleason Inverrary near Fort Lauderdale, Florida. For the next two months the tour stayed mostly in the southeast, except for the past winners who took off for the Tournament of Champions in California. Three Texas tournaments, starting with the Byron Nelson Classic, were played back-to-back in May, after which everyone moved east. For the next couple of months the players edged up the East Coast through the Carolinas, Philadelphia and into the Midwest.

After the St. Louis Children's Classic in July the schedule began to hopscotch. First to Canada, then to New York for the Westchester. The PGA Championship, especially for the rabbit, was out of the question, so he and his fellow tourists stayed around the northeast for the USI in Sutton, Mass. At that point the trouble began.

No wonder the rabbits and just about every other pro who hadn't already pocketed $50,000 for the year are irritated at the PGA scheduling committee. During the next four tournaments alone the pros had to travel more than 4000 miles: USI—Liggett and Myers in North Carolina—Sammy Davis in Connecticut—Southern Open in Georgia. Then there was that three-week period between September 20 and October 7: the B.C. Open in New York—Quad Cities in Iowa—Ohio Kings in Cincinnati. After that the tour went out to California for the Kaiser, down to Texas for the San Antonio, and finally to the World Open in North Carolina, and the Disney in Florida.

The PGA, taking its customary stance in loving the tournament sponsors more than the pros, says it has no control over the scheduling, which translated means it will back down if the sponsors resist. The one concession the scheduling committee gives to the pros, if a concession at all, is that the going doesn't get really rough until halfway through the year, by which time the players should have a little money in their pockets. Certainly enough, figures the PGA, to do some extra traveling.

Like most things about the tour, the schedule caters to the top pros, who can afford to fly from one stop to the next. Most of them take commercial jets. Palmer flies his own, and it's a kick to see him in United Airlines commercials saying it's the only way to travel. Sometimes, however, even the fliers have trouble. They've all experienced that sinking sensation of having a flight suddenly canceled. "I'm sorry, sir," an airline official would say, "but we've developed mechanical trouble on your flight to San Antonio. The next one leaves tomorrow morning at six fifteen. Here's $30. The airport motel is right over there and the restaurant is on the main floor. Good luck."

Mechanical trouble? Of course. Financial mechanics. It's just not worth it to haul eight people from Las Vagas to San Antonio.

Rabbits don't fly. They and other struggling players use their cars. Some drive all the time, even coast to coast, and by the time they get to the next tournament (where they have to register on Sunday for the Monday qualifier) they're dead tired. After all that they still have to find a place to stay. Not always an easy task, since the rabbit doesn't know whether he'll be in town all week. Even if he qualifies on Monday, he can't be sure he'll make the cut on Friday. To add to his misery it's necessary to make reservations well in advance, and many motels won't accept them without a deposit.

Mason Rudolph, on the tour fifteen years, ran into just such a problem at the PGA last year. "I have a terrible motel room," he said, apparently not making much of an impression on his innkeeper. "When I made my reservation I had to send a check for the week's rent in advance. That's the first time that has ever happened to me. I didn't like the trend."

The more popular pros don't have to worry about such things. There are usually Holiday and Ramada Inn representatives at tournaments to ask the big hitters if they would like a room at future tournaments. The stars often get them for free. What Holiday Inn wouldn't like to be able to put on its marquee "Welcome Jack Nicklaus"?

The not-so-well-known pros face other problems, such as skyrocketing prices. One motel in Houston upped its room price for the tournament week from $14 to $35 a day. Another hassle is getting close enough to the course so the player can grab a short nap between the round and the driving range. When Grier Jones was a rookie, he and his roommate, Jerry Heard, sometimes found themselves half an hour away from the course. And in some cases it's not unusual to find climbing out of a back seat, with blurry eyes and aching bones, a young player who the night before had given up on trying to find a place.

But even if he had found one, what's the big deal? "All the Holiday Inns look alike," says New York *Post* writer Sheila Moran, who used to travel with her rookie ex-husband on the tour, "except some are orange and some are blue. We'd sometimes wake up in a place and forget where we were. There's a real sameness to those places, week after week after week."

Dwaine Knight and his wife, Linda, stay away from the chain motels with their plastic food and American Gaudy decor, and instead look for places with kitchenettes, where they can cook their own food and snack it up in the middle of the night. If there's no kitchenette, a small cabin is their next choice. For those occasions they carry a small stove, utensils, and a couple of pots. "You have to economize," says Linda, "when you're not winning very much."

During the rabbit's first year he'll meet a number of people who'll invite him over to dinner or, perhaps, to spend the week at their home. When he comes back to town the following year his friends will be there with the same offer. But that situation mostly happens to single guys; when some of them have returned the next time with wives and children they're still invited over for dinner. As for staying over . . . well. That's why it's a good idea to make a motel reservation.

The players in the higher income brackets don't concern themselves with motels or a friend's extra bedroom. They rent a home for the week. At the PGA both Nicklaus and Palmer were said to have laid out $1000 a piece for nearby castles.

If the conditions are not the greatest, if the cost is ridiculously high, or even if you have to camp out in the back seat, the real factor that makes or breaks tour life off the course are the people you run into.

This is Dwaine Knight talking: "I remember last year at a Holiday Inn up in Elmsford, New York. I'll never forget it. I had just finished the tournament and was getting ready to leave. I was in the lobby with my bags and up comes this guy, a porter or something, and he was drunk. He started handling my clothes and wasn't doing such a good job, so I told him, 'Listen, just leave them alone and I'll take care of them.' Next thing I know we're having a big fight right there in the middle of everything. He wasn't going to give me my clothes, and he started putting them into a closet, into his little room somewhere in the back. You know, he was really off his rocker. It took the manager and everybody else to get my clothes away from this guy so I could put them in the car."

Where else but New York?

"Miami," says Grier Jones. "I couldn't leave my room. If I went outside, they would have run me over. They're crazy down there."

Most pros, being from the South and West as they are, have never gotten used to the ragtag, helter-skelter life in the urban North, or in any big city for that matter. Except for riding to and

from the course and an occasional meal at a restaurant they stay
pretty much to themselves. Cities like New York, Detroit, Chicago,
and Miami are like giant leviathans ready to devour them. The
lifestyle is foreign to them, the pace too hectic and the people too
much in a hurry to extend the courtesy they've been accustomed to
in their home towns.

If it weren't for having to go there for a tournament, chances
are most pros would scratch big cities off their itineraries forever.
When it was suggested that the cities were just another real-life
experience, they would respond, "Your life, maybe. Not mine."

New York is to Albuquerque, Dwaine Knight's home town,
what major championships are to smaller ones. Big affairs like the
Open and the PGA are played on different courses and run by
different people each year, while less prestigious ones like the
Greater Greensborough and Kemper Opens and the Philadelphia
Classic have been held in the same place for years. That makes a
big difference, particularly in the way the players are treated.

"Without hurting anybody's feeling and being right truth-
ful," says Grier Jones, "every-week tournaments are much better
run by far. They treat the players so much nicer and they have just
so much more experience doing the little things like, oh, a baby-
sitting service. Some of the tournaments have the service right
there on the course, then your wife can follow you around. And
they have a little lunch for you in the afternoon."

We were sitting in the Canterbury clubhouse and Grier nodded to his right. "You go in there and have a sandwich and a coke."

There's also the comforting feeling of meeting the same people
year after year, of saying hello and exchanging stories about past
years and performances. Where there's a sense of tradition, which
the players remember from their home clubs, they feel more at
home. What distinguished the U.S. Open at Oakmont, where
everyone was racing back and forth, half confused and half nervous, and The Masters, which management-consulting firms ought
to use as a model of efficiency and charm, is in the organization, the
attention to detail, and the attempts to make the players as comfortable as possible.

Despite the congeniality, the friendships, and the exposure to every conceivable lifestyle from one end of the country to the other, traveling on the professional tour is little more than bouncing from one town to the next. The pro who's been on the tour for awhile —and the one who wants to be—eats, sleeps, talks about, puts all his energy into, and dreams about one thing. His game. Those not willing to put that much into it get the message pretty quickly.

It's a lonely trip. No one but the player himself, once he gets out on the course, can put it all together. Outside interests like a lot of women and booze are out of the question. The ones who swing all night and then expect to swing all day are gone after a few months. Culturally, the pro lives in a vacuum. News from the outside world comes via the 11 o'clock news, if he isn't already in bed. When Vladimir in *Waiting for Godot* says his life consists of "waiting for waiting," he may just as well have been talking about the golf pro whose existence is as insulated.

The vast majority of them marry young, out of love and to keep their sanity. Of the top 30 money winners in 1973 only the mysterious Mr. X, Miller Barber, who disappears every night, was single. The rest of them need the companionship after a rough day on the course, someone to share their ups and downs.

Grier Jones didn't bring his wife and kid along in his rookie year because he didn't feel he could afford to. When he made the top 60 and some money he brought them out. "My wife walking around the course with me, or not walking with me, makes little difference," he says. "I just like to have her around at night, you know, because it gives me something to do. Or if I go to a cocktail party, I feel out of place just standing there. I like to have her there because she kind of talks and makes me feel good."

The sameness of the living conditions have even extended to the players' habits. Linda Knight, who has been traveling with Dwaine for less then a year, says, "Everybody's just kind of on the same level. I guess golf puts them there, too, because sure, a lot of people have nicer cars and stuff, but out there on the course everybody's right together. You know, they even tie their neckties the same and get dressed the same. And it's kind of neat, you know, because it's not like you were in school or working—where one person wears a $300 dress and somebody else wears a $30 dress. Some may have more than others, but their attitudes aren't imposed upon you that way. I haven't met too many people who feel better than you, everybody's just kind of struggling along."

Sheila Moran has a different impression of married life. "Sometimes it's a strain because you don't have much privacy. There's nowhere to go by yourself, except maybe the bathroom. You have to make awfully sure the two of you are compatible. Spending twenty-four hours a day, every day, is difficult." But oddly enough, in this day of short-term marriages and quicky separations, in the last five years there have been no more than a dozen divorces on the tour.

One reason for that has to do with the nature of the golfer himself. Conservative, stable, he's the Tory in a sportsworld of Whigs. "Maybe conservative isn't really a good word," Dwaine Knight disagreed, "maybe we're not as flamboyant. We play four straight days a week and practice or travel the rest. So there isn't the breaking action of a football player who plays once a week. He can go out Monday and raise hell. Even baseball players who have a four-game stand get a three-day break. And also we're not on a team; we're basically on our own. We can't afford to raise hell."

The Monday afternoon canvas is painted with one of two colors for the professional golf tour rabbit. Golden yellow or gray. Whether or not the sun is shining, for the ones who have qualified, the day is bright. For those who haven't, it might as well be night, the gloom is that thick.

The non-qualifier has a lot of problems, not least of which is that he competes only once a week. And since the Monday events offer no purses, he's also in the hole.

There is a bad taste left in the non-qualifier's mouth when he leaves that Monday. It has to do with those who are exempt from having to qualify for the major events. There are 144 players in each tournament, and some say a few of them have no business being there.

Golfers exempt from having to qualify for regular events on the 1973 tour fell into one or more of these categories:

1. All former PGA and U.S. Open champions. Prior to 1970 they received lifetime exemptions. Those since 1970 received ten-year exemptions only.

2. Current British Open champion.

3. Leading players in tour-point system for 1970–71–72 and leading money winners of 1968–69. The leading money winner was exempted prior to 1970 for the following five years. Since then, the leader in a tour-point system based mostly on earnings gets his exemption.

4. Members of the 1971 American Ryder Cup team.

5. Members of the 1971 British Ryder Cup team (limit of three events).

6. Winners of major tour events during the twelve-month period prior to the tournament involved.

7. The 60 leading pros in tour-point standings for 1972 (based almost entirely on earnings).

8. Players finishing 72 holes in the event immediately preceding the tournament involved.

9. Previous winners of the tournament involved. Those winners previous to 1970 got lifetime exemptions for the event. Those since receive ten-year exemptions only.

10. The low 25 scorers in the previous year of the tournament involved.

11. Four PGA members from the local section of the tournament involved (club professionals only), as selected by the section and approved by the tournament sponsor.

12. The local PGA section champion.

13. PGA Club Professional National Champion (limit of three events).

14. Head pro or designated assistant at the club involved.

15. A player-director of the Tournament Players Division

taking office after October 1, 1972, who shall have served a two-year term as such a director.

16. Eight players invited by the sponsor of the tournament involved.

17. Beginning in 1974 the 50 career money winners of the tour are exempt.

Of the 144-player field, about 125 fall into one of those categories, leaving 20 or so qualifiers to the other spots.

The objections:

Rule Numbers 1 (Previous PGA and U.S. Open champs), 9 (All previous winners of tournament involved), and 17 (top 50 career money winners). Let's say a number of men who fit into one of these exemptions decide to enter a tournament. The field cannot go above 144, which means those players who are not normally exempt—the rabbits—will (if there are any slots open) fight it out over another 18 holes.

Frank Beard says the "top 50 winner" rule is a good one because he would hate to see "a Dan Sikes or an Art Wall tangling with unproven tour fledglings in those ghastly Monday qualifying rounds." It seems the rule was made for Wall and Sikes, who, without it, would not have been able to play on the 1974 tour.

Professional golf may be the only major sport promoting mediocrity in its ranks. Wall and Sikes used to be top players—not anymore—and there are a lot of qualifiers who played better and won more last year and either continued their qualifying rounds or had their cards pulled. Rookie Gary Sanders is a case in point.

There are five criteria a first-year player must meet in order to keep his card. He must enter at least 15 tournaments (Sanders entered 32); he must qualify for half of those he enters (Sanders qualified in 23); he must make the cut in one-third of those he qualifies for (he made the cut in eight); he must maintain a scoring average of 74 or better (he averaged 73.6); and he must make at least $3000 in official tournament money, not including the second tour. Sanders won only $1,481.48. His total for the year was $3,390, including second-tour money. But the PGA does not consider the second tour official. If it weren't for a little finagling around with the PGA, who finally let him enter two more tournaments, he would have lost his card. As it turned out, he pocketed $2475 at the Phoenix Open and kept it.

Established players like Bob Rosberg, George Bayer, R. H. Sikes, and Ken Venturi were among those who made less than Sanders. In fact those four tour standbys made less money in 1973 than 23 of 25 TPD qualifying rookies and fell below them in the other categories as well.

It hardly seems fair for these golfers to take up spots a rookie should fill, especially when the veterans hardly ever make the cut.

In other sports when a player hits the skids the teams can't afford to keep him around. They send him to the minors where he has to climb back up, or release him. In golf, meanwhile, some old-timers are taking spots away from young stars who can beat them all day long.

Another rule that irritates the rookies is Number 16, the one allowing the tournament sponsor eight positions. The chances for the tour veteran getting in on this one are also good, but more often then not another faction gets the nod, the amateurs. At the 1973 Hartford Open some sponsors' slots were filled with amateurs, but the real killer for the rookies came when two regulars couldn't make it. Their positions were also given to the non-pros. They could just as well have gone to rookies who are, after all, paying their way and trying to make a living. The TPD and PGA don't seem to care too much about that, though; they're more concerned about spicing up the field with name amateurs.

A rule not appearing on the list, but which no one likes, concerns qualifying on Friday. The TPD School graduate whose card is pulled in December hates the rule because he's not eligible to compete, even on Friday. Joe Schwendeman puts it this way: "Those TPD members who were terminated in December usually skip this year. But there's a catch. Some of them can play because they are PGA members."

The only problem there is that a TPD cardholder must have

the card four years before he's eligible to join the PGA. "We have this thing written into our regulations," Schwendeman continued. "If you are a PGA member and not a member of TPD, you may pay us a $25 limited membership each week and enter that tournament as a PGA member."

How does one got to be one of 6000 PGA members? Serve an apprenticeship and become a teaching pro. About the Friday qualifier, Joe? "It means these fellows have to play 18 on Friday, and the top 20 percent of the field are allowed to come back on Monday and go against all the regular TPD members. So, in effect, they have to play 36 holes just to get into the regular tournament. And that bugs them."

To keep the non-qualifier somewhat alive, a few years ago the PGA came up with the Second Tour, a series of small-money tournaments running concurrently with the big ones. In 1973 there were 24 of them paying the winners just under $60,000. The major problem has to do with promotion. "To be realistic about the whole thing," says Schwendeman, "it's mighty tough to sell these events. The Second Tour sponsors do not know who's playing in them until the Monday qualifier is over, and consequently the sponsors can't publicize who'll be in them. So it's a problem getting them to say they'll put up $10,000 for nobody."

Schwendeman says something should be done about this, but so far neither he nor anyone else in the PGA has come up with an answer. One solution might be to offer sponsorships to companies for a reduced rate and then contact the local papers whose sportswriters are always hungry for news. The pros playing on the second tour are the future stars of the regular tour, and each of them has a story worth telling. Galleries would attend these events if they knew they existed. Thus far the second tour has been given little or no coverage.

If there is no Second Tour event, however, the rabbit stashes his family and clubs in the car and takes off for the next town and the next tournament. The non-qualifiers spend their whole lives living one week ahead of schedule.

But even when he arrives at the next site he sometimes has to contend with club officials who refuse to let him practice. Dwaine Knight doesn't like to arrive too early "because a lot of places don't like you, particularly if you're a rabbit. Their courses are taken up for a whole week by the big pros, so the clubs don't like a rabbit coming in, chopping up their tees and greens. That really doesn't happen, but they want to believe it does."

If some courses don't allow playing, many of them let the rabbit walk off the yardages. Armed with a little notebook he writes down the distances and draws little pictures of the greens. Every once in a while the club will allow him to play in a foursome with three members. That way the club doesn't think the young pro is taking up much room. "But I'll never forget the Byron Nelson at Dallas," Dwaine recalls. "They wouldn't let us do anything, not even walk it. There were only nine spots for 80-odd guys. I was fortunate and made it, but they wouldn't even let us use the putting greens after the qualifying rounds. It was really unreasonable. Things like this happen, things people never hear about."

As the non-qualifier slithers off into the horizon, the qualifier, the one who'll play on Thursday, gets ready.

Tuesday

Since many Monday qualifying rounds are not played on the tournament course, the rookie should know about the layout he's going to be confronting. He picks up his caddie and plays a "map-off" round. The yardage, the hazards, distances from trees, sprinkler heads, the pitch and roll of the greens are all jotted down in his notebook. He hasn't got the advantage of the other pros who have played the course in years past. Everything's new, especially himself.

Wednesday

Pro-Am day is usually off-limits for the rabbit because the celebrities, businessmen, and club members would rather play with a pro they've at least heard of. Dwaine Knight and other first-year players often sign up for Pro-Am day as alternates, in case some of the popular pros don't feel like playing.

Wednesday consists mostly of time on the driving range and practice green, but it can suddenly turn into another day on the course if the rabbit's name is called.

Most pros are not wild about playing in pro-ams because they have to contend with terrible players who slow the game up and good ones who think they know it all. In *Pro* Frank Beard says the scratch-to-five handicap player is the toughest to play with. "First, and foremost, he wants to beat the pro. That's all he cares about, not the team or anything else. Second, if he can't beat the pro, he wants to keep his own score (which doesn't mean a thing in a pro-am) and impress the pro with occasional totals. . . . But when the low handicapper tells his friends he was only two strokes behind Arnold Palmer or was two strokes ahead of Frank Beard, he doesn't mention that he was hitting from up front by the ladies' tee and was getting a lot of putts conceded to him and was in a non-pressure situation."

The rookie doesn't worry about such things; he's more interested in getting some extra money. He's already been guaranteed a fee and expenses for playing in the first place, and hopes to place in the top 15 pros or top five pro-am teams, where he'll make a little more.

The most important thing, though, is getting to play the course one more time before the tournament begins the next day.

Thursday

It's called the box, a small tent located by the first and tenth tees where ten young players sit and wait. They talk about the course, gab about how their games are coming, watch the galleries parade by. But most of all they hope one or more of the players drop out of the tournament so they, the alternates, get a chance to play.

The alternates are rabbits who failed by one stroke to qualify the Monday before but have been given another chance. Slim as the chance is it's better than nothing. The first three or four alternates will probably get in, but as they get on down the list the hope fades.

It's a sweaty, frustrating existence in that tent. At the Dow Jones three years ago a rumor was spreading that one pro had a sore back and wouldn't play. It was a half rumor as it turned out when the pro stood up on the first tee, hit his drive and began walking down the fairway. He pulled out an iron to hit his second shot and was suddenly wracked with pain. He withdrew from the tournament. The alternate who was supposed to take his place slammed his hand hard against his bench. The rule states if a player hits the first ball he is officially in the event and cannot be replaced that day.

Then there was the time at the Shrine-Robinson Open in Illinois when John Wells was first alternate and waited in the box all day long. Nothing happened so he began driving to the next tournament. The next morning's paper reported seven withdrawals after the opening day. That rule says a player may be replaced on the day after his withdrawal.

The alternate is in the odd position of waiting at one tournament for the chance to replace a pro while he might be playing just a few miles away in one of the Second Tour events. The decision is a difficult one, but as most of them will tell you, playing on the big tour is what they're after, so they might as well do their time in the box.

The players who did qualify will most likely not be seen by many people on the first day because the folks who make up the pairings don't make it possible. The rabbit tees off very early in the morning, when dew is still on the ground, or in the middle of the afternoon, when the course has already been trampled by the field. He will not play with a Nicklaus or Trevino. The pairings, like everything else on the tour, depend upon performance. Past champions are put together, then the exempt players, and last the rabbits. The reason for this is simple: the gallery has not paid to see Slim Jones who made $1.20 last year.

Friday

The big days for the qualifiers are Monday, Thursday and Friday. After spending two or three months on the tour they develop an attitude they admit is potentially very dangerous. Instead of teeing off Thursday with the idea of winning the tournament, the foremost thought in their minds is making the Friday cut. For most of them the tournament is a two-day affair, and as a result they're often cautious, easing up on shots, playing each other rather than the course itself.

"Thursday and Friday *is* the tournament," says Dwaine Knight. "If you make the cut you stay; if you don't it's all the way down the road to the next place to qualify again on Monday. And, boy, missing the cut really puts a time limit on you, because you have to get to the next place to register on Sunday."

Gary Sanders put it this way: "I seem to play my best on Monday. My practice rounds Tuesday were not quite as good, and by Thursday I was getting worse. Friday I knew I wasn't going to play well. It got so bad my wife Linda started packing Friday so we could move on to the next town."

Saturday

The pressure is on. On this day, for the first time in the tournament, the rabbit becomes a threat. If his two rounds have put him in contention, he may be paired up with one of the big hitters and get his face on national TV. For the rookie who makes the cut this is the only time he gets to see guys like Weiskopf and Nicklaus close up. Otherwise, they may as well be on the opposite sides of the world.

In the military the caste system runs according to rank; the generals don't hang around with the lieutenants, the lieutenants don't fraternize with the sergeants, and so on. Golf's caste system works the same way. Except on the playing field or on the practice tee for a lesson, the big-time pros and their families have little to do with the underlings.

"There seems to be a big wall between us, a class barrier," says Linda Knight, "and until you break through the wall you don't know what the big pros are doing. It's not so much hard feeling, but I've seen it during a practice round when, say, there are two rookies behind four big pros. They make the rookies wait, won't let them play through."

There have been other small but significant things that help to promote the separateness. When lesser-known players have walked up to a Coke stand and asked the guy for something to drink, the player often gets charged or told there isn't anything left. Five minutes later a name pro will walk up and be served for free.

That's not to say, however, that the top players won't help the rookies. Billy Casper and Lee Trevino have been particularly helpful to Dwaine Knight by helping him with his game and mental attitude. Gary Player is known as one of the nicest guys on the tour and one of the first to offer suggestions to the younger pros.

There is one man who, although making major contributions to the game itself, has not endeared himself to most of the younger players. Former TPD Commissioner Joe Dey.

One of the first gripes about Dey happened back in 1949 when Doug Ford wanted to play in the British Open as amateur. Dey was USGA Executive Secretary at the time and was investigating Ford's expenses.

"Coming up to the Open," recalls Ford, "he kept refusing to tell me whether I was eligible as an amateur. I finally got hot, tore up my entry as an amateur and declared myself a pro. In those days a new pro could play in only three tournaments for money and then couldn't accept a check for six months. So I played in the Open, the Motor City and the Canadian Open and then had to lay out a half year."

More recently there have been bitches about Dey's attitude toward the rabbits. "He has no compassion for the rookies out there," said one pro. "He'll walk up to the big names, but if there is a rookie right next to him he won't even acknowledge him."

There is an argument that Dey does not have time to meet individually with every pro. Most people agree with that, saying that he doesn't know ten rookies by name. Jack Tuthill, TPD Tournament Director, is the opposite. "He's just the nicest guy in the world," says another rookie, "and he's concerned about everybody. He comes up and asks how you're doing. Let's say a pro has been shooting above par every week, but he's improving, practicing a lot. Jack Tuthill will walk up to him on the practice tee and give him encouragement. He knows everybody by name."

An example of the difference between the two men came in 1973 when Dwaine Knight, who had been on the tour for a few months, broke his hand when a car door was slammed on it. He was out for five months and consequently didn't earn enough to keep his player's card. Each pro is supposed to be given a full year to make the cut. Dwaine's card was pulled in December and was told he wouldn't be able to compete until the following July. He called Dey, who refused to talk to him. "He was too busy and wouldn't even refer me to someone who could help. I called Jack Tuthill and within a matter of hours he got to Dey and my card was restored."

Another incident happened at the USI Classic in Sutton, Mass. Pro Jim King of Miami was suspended from the tour for one year and given a $1000 fine by Dey for allegedly striking a PGA official. "It has been determined," said Dey, "that Mr. King cursed PGA Tournament Players' Division Pete Sesso, grabbed Mr. Sesso's throat in a threatening manner, and choked Mr. Sesso."

That was Dey's story. There were others. According to one pro who asked not to be mentioned by name—"I might get called in for it"—Sesso had been bugging King during the entire round, telling him to tuck his shirt in and not to talk so much. "He really nagged him. I couldn't believe it. I probably would have shot him. Jim didn't actually strike Sesso. He screamed at him and told him he'd push him into the gallery if he didn't leave him alone. I mean, Jim was playing for money and that guy was throwing his game off. I don't know why Sesso was after him, but there was no excuse for it."

Dey has since been replaced as Commissioner by Deane Beman, a much younger man who has played on the tour. Everyone's waiting to see how he'll work out.

Late Saturday afternoon and the rookie suddenly finds himself in contention, tied for the lead. He checks the next day's pairings and finds himself playing with Nicklaus and John Schlee, number ten on the '73 money list.

When our rookie wakes up the next morning his wife tells him he's tossed and turned a lot during the night.

Sunday

When he gets out to the course he's met friends and fellow pros who wish him the best of luck. His first confrontation comes a few seconds later when a dozen reporters begin shooting questions at him: "How do you feel? Whaddya think about the course? You ever play with Nicklaus before? Was the 66 yesterday your best on the tour?"

He remembers from players school that lecture on how to meet the press: Tell 'em what you like over what you don't like about the tournament and the course; talk about your game, they like that; be cordial, try to remember the writers' names; smile; and the most important thing.

What?

Don't get shook.

At the first tee he finds his caddie is as surprised as the rookie that he's tied for first. The caddie has carried a lot of bags for rookies, most of whom never saw Saturday morning. This kid, though, has a shot, long as he doesn't get rattled.

The rookie stands by the back tees and looks down the first fairway. The gallery, like huge undulating snakes, weaves down both sides to the green. The first time he felt their presence was late yesterday afternoon when word must have gotten back that an unknown was knocking hell out of par. But it was nothing like this. He recalls what Hale Irwin said about playing with Palmer and Crampton in the Western Open. "I felt I was getting in the way of Bruce and Arnold," Irwin said. "Playing with Palmer is something else. His fans don't pay attention to the other guys." The rookie remembers other pros talking about how the big galleries are made up mostly of star watchers who hardly know anything about the game. They stampede, get in your way, knock you down.

But he knows something else, too. Ever since high school he's emulated Nicklaus, who is standing on the other side of the tee talking with some officials. He's in awe of the man, but he feels good about playing with someone great; it'll get his own game up.

Schlee's first up and belts his drive down the right side about 290 out. Schlee's been on the tour since 1965 and had his best year in 1973 with one win, two seconds and over $118,000 in the bank. But he's best known as the tour's resident astrologer. You can find him hunched over a player's chart, calculating how the player's doing, why he's doing it, and what he'll be doing in the future. Just like a Gemini, Schlee's sign, the dual personality, one the disciplined golfer, the other off in the stars somewhere.

Nicklaus booms his drive down the center.

For the last five hours the rookie has been concentrating on fusing the mechanical and mental parts of his game together. He's been doing it for years and here's where it's got to pay off. He's stood in front of the mirror a thousand times and watched his swing, breaking his wrists a little higher on the backswing, playing his irons a little higher on the left, shortening his grip. And out on the driving range, where he used Hogan's old method of pretending he was behind a tree and hitting shots over and around it.

The marshals hold up QUIET PLEASE signs as the rookie tees up his ball. His driver starts back, arching high, and then whistles down and through the ball. The follow-through brings his head up and he sees the Spaulding Dot sailing down the right side and begin drawing to the left.

Applause. A smile forms at the corners of his mouth. Safe!

His second shot to the green has left him eight feet from the hole. His opponents have both sunk their putts for pars. He remembers all that psycho-cybernetic stuff he and his wife have read together. Think *mental,* tell yourself the putt will drop! Don't *wonder* if it will, *know* it will!

His Bullseye blade connects solidly with the ball. It's about a six-inch break, left to right. The ball climbs slightly. The green is fast. The gallery is silent. Breaking down . . . in!

Things look good by the seventh hole, a par three, a hundred-eighty-five yards away. Trapped on both sides and with a giant bunker up front. Just like the greenskeeper to set the pin twenty feet behind the big trap. The rookie has a short talk with his caddie.

"Four iron, would you say?"

The caddie takes a look at the green; he's clubbed the kid right so far, specially back on four with the seven iron four feet from the pin. "I don't know," he tells the rookie, "you got some wind behind you."

"I'd hate to be short."

"Me too."

He pulls out the four and walks to the tee. Up to this point he's been playing aggressive. No time to switch now. The ball gets off clean, and except for a little too much loft it covers the flag all the way, hits twenty-five feet behind, gets some spin, and rolls back. Twelve feet away. Ten minutes later he sinks for the bird.

At the turn Nicklaus is two under for the day, nine for the tournament. Schlee had some trouble with his long irons and has come off nine with a two over 38, putting him four behind Nicklaus and five behind the leader—the rookie—who steps up to ten, his lucky number. He is now 10 under and getting nervous.

The news comes on fourteen. By this time he has two shareholders for the lead. Bruce Crampton birdied sixteen and seventeen, and Tom Weiskopf picked up an eagle three on fifteen. Nicklaus and four others are just one back.

The information has done its job as the rookie pushes a six iron into the right trap. On the next shot his sand wedge leaves the ball thirty tough feet from the hole. The ball breaks twice over two hogbacks. It looks impossible. He can't tell what will happen for the first twenty feet as the putt seems to sway back and forth on its way toward the cup. But the last ten feet are a cinch. Unless a major catastrophe hits, he's got it.

Clunk! It's still a three-way tie.

The seventeenth is one of those holes that plays like a dream; either all good or all bad. At three hundred eighty yards, it looks like a breeze from every conceivable angle but the golfer's as he sees what his second shot has to do. All three golfers have used three woods off the tee to avoid the small lake in the middle of the fairway, about two hundred eighty yards out.

The rookie approaches his ball, off on the right side of the fairway, just in the rough. He's got a good lie; the ball is sitting up on the grass. The only thing he's got to worry about is the right bunker and getting the ball into the green that looks, from where he is standing, like the bottom of a dish, surrounded on three sides by sloping hills and in the back by a TV tower and a few thousand excited fans.

He has another talk with his caddie. "How far is it?"

"One twenty?"

"You tellin' or askin'?"

"Could be a little more."

The rookie pulls out his notebook and turns to the yardage on seventeen. "Let's see," he thinks out loud. "I was about this far on Thursday and I hit a wedge. Left me long."

"On the back edge." The caddie remembers it, and the putt that stopped an inch short.

"Well, looks like another wedge today, whaddya think?"

"I'd say."

Out comes the club, the caddie picks up the bag and steps out of the way.

There were two things the rookie should have remembered before hitting that wedge; one of them was something Casper told him about playing percentage golf; and the other had to do with not changing his game, especially when he's tied for the lead with two holes to go. When you're hitting into a green like this, Casper said to him, you have a much better chance rolling it up with a seven iron than trying to make it stop on a dime with a wedge. Your percentages are much better. The second piece of advice the rookie should have remembered had come up earlier in the day. When you're playing good aggressive golf, don't ease up.

He hit the wedge and held back. The ball dropped into the trap. Buried. Three shots later the rookie was still putting for a double bogey six, a two-footer he almost missed.

His bogey on eighteen didn't help matters much. When all the scores were in he found himself alone in seventh place.

The end of the world? Hardly, even though the two shots on seventeen cost him $7000 and the bogey on eighteen another $4000. He learned a lot in that expensive lesson. When he teed it up at the following Monday qualifier he had begun to climb out of the rabbit stew.

Bibliography

Bartlett, Michael, (ed), *Bartlett's World Golf Encyclopedia,* New York, Bantam Books, Inc., 1973. History, anecdotes, and statistics of the game.

Jenkins, Dan, *The Dogged Victims of Inexorable Fate,* Boston, Little, Brown and Co., 1970. Stories of the trials and tribulations a golfer experiences with his game.

McCormack, Mark H., *The Wonderful World of Professional Golf,* New York, Atheneum Publishers, 1973. A history of the pro tour by the manager of Palmer, Nicklaus, and others.

Schapp, Dick, *Pro: Frank Beard on the Golf Tour,* New York, World Publishing Co., 1970. A day-by-day account of Beard's experiences on the 1969 tour.

Wind, Herbert W., (ed), New York, Simon and Schuster, 1954. Series of articles on most aspects of the game.